20 EVENTS

Explorers

WHO FOUND NEW WORLDS

DALE ANDERSON

RSVP

**RAINTREE
STECK-VAUGHN**
PUBLISHERS
The Steck-Vaughn Company

Austin, Texas

Consultant: Gary Gerstle, Department of History, The Catholic University of America

Developed for Steck-Vaughn Company by
Visual Education Corporation, Princeton, New Jersey

Project Director: Jewel Moulthrop
Assistant Editor: Emilie McCardell
Researcher: Carol Ciaston
Photo Research: Photosearch, Inc.
Production Supervisor: Maryellen Filipek
Proofreading Management: Amy Davis
Word Processing: Cynthia C. Feldner
Interior Design: Lee Grabarczyk
Cover Design: Maxson Crandall
Page Layout: Maxson Crandall, Lisa R. Evans

Raintree Steck-Vaughn Publishers staff

Editor: Shirley Shalit
Project Manager: Joyce Spicer

Library of Congress Cataloging-in-Publication Data

Anderson, Dale, 1953–
    Explorers who found new worlds / Dale Anderson
        p.   cm. — (20 Events)
    Includes bibliographical references and index.
    Summary: Describes the journeys of twenty explorers who opened up new worlds, from Marco Polo to Roald Amundsen.
    ISBN 0-8114-4931-9
    1. Explorers—Juvenile literature.   [1. Explorers.]   I. Title.
II. Series.
G175.A53 1994   93–19016
910′.92—dc20   CIP
                                                                  AC

Printed and bound in the United States

    2 3 4 5 6 7 8 9 0   VH   99 98 97 96 95 94

Cover: Although Coronado (inset) did not find the gold he sought, he and other Spanish explorers left their mark. Cities grew around the Spanish missions founded in South America, Mexico, and the American Southwest.

Credits and Acknowledgments

Cover photos: John Cancalosi/Stock Boston (background), The Bettmann Archive (inset)
Illustrations: American Composition and Graphics
Maps: Parrot Graphics

4: Giraudon/Art Resource, N.Y.; **5:** The Bettmann Archive (left), Carl Purcell/Photo Researchers, Inc. (right); **6:** Metropolitan Museum of Art (left), Rare Books and Manuscripts Division, New York Public Library, Astor, Lenox and Tilden Foundations (right); **8:** Museu Nacional de Arte, Antiqua, Portugal (left), Library of Congress (right); **9:** Robert Fried/Stock Boston; **10:** Library of Congress (top), Lee Boltin (bottom); **11:** Kenneth Murray/Photo Researchers, Inc.; **12:** Library of Congress (left), Michael Dwyer/Stock Boston (right); **13:** Courtesy of The John Carter Brown Library, at Brown University; **15:** John Cancalosi/Stock Boston (top), The Bettmann Archive (bottom); **16:** Neg. #15106. Photo: J. Kirschner, Courtesy Department Library Services, American Museum of Natural History (left), Reproduced by permission of The Huntington Library, San Marino, California (right); **17:** Will and Deni McIntyre/Photo Researchers, Inc.; **18:** The Bettmann Archive (left), Library of Congress (right); **19:** Ted Spiegel; **20:** The Bettmann Archive; **21:** John Elk III/Stock Boston; **22:** Library of Congress (left), *LaSalle Erecting a Cross and Taking Possession of the Land, March 1682,* 1847/8. © 1993 National Gallery of Art, Washington, Paul Mellon Collection (right); **24:** The Bettmann Archive; **25:** Visual Education Corporation (top), The Smithsonian Institution, National Museum of Natural History (bottom); **26:** © National Maritime Museum London; **27:** © National Maritime Museum London; **29:** Government of Canada, ISTC (left), National Gallery of Canada, Ottawa. Transfer from the Canadian War Memorials, 1921 (right); **30:** Independence National Historic Park Collection (top left and right), Reproduced by permission of The Huntington Library, San Marino, California (bottom); **32:** The Bettmann Archive; **33:** George Holton/Photo Researchers, Inc.; **34:** Royal Geographical Society, London (bottom left and right); **35:** Royal Geographical Society, London; **36:** New York Public Library, Astor, Lenox and Tilden Foundations (left), Australian News and Information Service (right); **37:** Ulrike Welsch/Photo Researchers, Inc.; **38:** George Turner/Photo Researchers, Inc. (top), Bettmann/Hulton (bottom); **39:** Owen Franken/Stock Boston; **40:** Library of Congress (left), Bettmann/Hulton (right); **41:** George Holton/Photo Researchers, Inc.; **42:** The Mansell Collection; **43:** Ira Kirschenbaum/Stock Boston

Contents

Marco Polo

Through descriptions of his travels in Asia, Marco Polo opened the eyes of Europeans to the riches of the East.

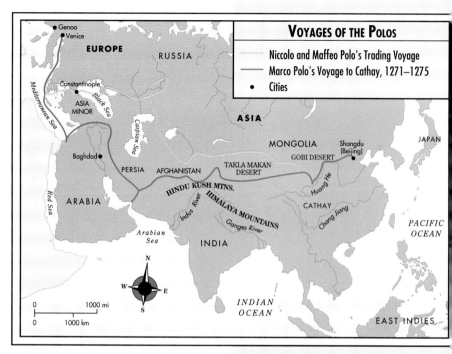

VOYAGES OF THE POLOS
- Niccolo and Maffeo Polo's Trading Voyage
- Marco Polo's Voyage to Cathay, 1271–1275
- • Cities

▲ Polo, his father, and his uncle traveled about 15,000 miles to China (then called Cathay) and back.

◀ The book about Marco Polo's travels to Cathay amazed Europeans with its marvelous accounts of Asia. Yet before his death, Polo said, "I did not write half of what I saw."

Land of Mystery

In the late 13th century, trade between Europe and Asia traveled on the famous Silk Road. This caravan trail from China to Constantinople (modern Istanbul) brought silk and spices from Asia. But the Asian route was controlled by Muslim traders. European merchants who plied the Mediterranean Sea could not trade directly with the East.

With contact blocked in this way, Europeans knew little about Asia. Some missionaries, who had traveled in the East to convert the Asians, reported back. But Asia remained a land of mystery, an unknown region. The Polo family changed that.

Marco Polo's father, Niccolò, and his uncle Maffeo were merchants from Venice. After a 14-year trading voyage, they returned to their city in 1269. In that time, they had traveled all the way to China, which was then called Cathay. There they met its ruler, Kublai Khan. Intrigued by the westerners, the khan had asked them to return to him with 100 learned men sent by the pope to discuss Christianity.

Marco Polo's Career

Unable to make arrangements with the pope but unwilling to wait any longer, the Polo brothers left for Asia again in 1271. They took with them Marco, who was only about 17 years old. He would be middle-aged when he finally returned to Venice.

Marco's Travels The party needed three or four years to reach Cathay. They crossed Asia Minor (present-day Turkey) and Persia (present-day Iraq and Iran). One year of the journey was spent in northern Afghanistan, perhaps recovering from malaria. They had to cross the Hindu Kush and Himalaya Mountains and the vast Takla Makan and Gobi deserts. At each new place, Marco gathered stories about the people and animals. Finally, they reached the khan's summer palace, called Shangdu (in present-day Beijing).

The Polos were fortunate to have arrived at this moment in Chinese history. Kublai Khan was a Mongol, not a Chinese. As a result, he was more willing to trust foreigners than a native Chinese emperor would have been.

The friendship and support of Kublai Khan enabled Polo to remain in Cathay for nearly 20 years and helped his family become very wealthy.

The Effect of Marco Polo

The effect of Marco Polo's book was electrifying. *Descriptions of the World* spread across Europe rapidly. Many people disbelieved some of the book—even parts that were true. They mistrusted the stories of money made of paper and of black stones that burned like wood (neither paper money nor coal was then used by Europeans). But people were enchanted by the accounts of the wealth of the East, the rich hoards of spices in the Indies, the pearls in India, and the gold in Japan—a land unknown to Europeans until then.

Europeans wanted some of this vast wealth. The desire to explore was awakened. It took almost 200 years, but by the end of the 15th century, Christopher Columbus had sailed from Spain to reach Japan and Vasco da Gama was leaving Portugal to reach India. Those voyages revealed worlds that even Marco Polo could never have imagined.

With his support, the Polos stayed in Cathay for 16 or 17 years. During that stay, Marco's father and uncle became rich. Marco himself seems to have become a favorite of the khan, in part, perhaps, because of his stories about the fascinating things he'd seen.

Marco also became a trusted official serving the emperor. He traveled extensively for Kublai Khan throughout Southeast Asia, reaching as far as India.

By 1290, the Polos were ready to return to Europe. Seeing the great khan age, they feared that they would lose their position when he died. They were also homesick. In 1292, they left Cathay. The voyage was long, and during it they learned of Kublai Khan's death. They returned to Venice 24 years after leaving.

Marco's Book Shortly afterward, a war erupted between Venice and another Italian city, Genoa, which ensured Marco Polo's place in history. Captured during that fighting, he entertained fellow prisoners with stories of his travels. A writer of romances named Rustichello heard these stories and convinced Polo to tell of his adventures in a book.

As Polo dictated, Rustichello took notes for the book. Either Polo, Rustichello, or both were not too concerned about facts or dates. The book contained many untruths, such as the story of Prester John, a mythical Christian king who supposedly ruled a wealthy land somewhere in Asia. Rustichello added strange details of his own invention. But the book also contained many keenly observed facts.

The Gobi Desert, with its swirling dunes, is much the same today as it was when crossed by the Polos.

Christopher Columbus

By landing in the Americas, Columbus paved the way for the European settlement of two continents.

This print, made almost 100 years after Columbus's first voyage, portrays the navigator bidding farewell to Ferdinand and Isabella—an event that probably did not occur.

No portraits painted of Columbus during his life have survived—although such a portrait may have been the model for this painting.

Two Worlds Apart

In 1492, the world known to Europeans was much smaller than it is now. They were familiar with their own continent and parts of Asia and Africa. But they knew nothing of the Americas—or of the people living there.

Centuries earlier, Asians had crossed a land bridge between Siberia and Alaska into what would become America. Over time, they spread throughout the two continents of the Western Hemisphere. When rising seas covered the land bridge, the peoples of the earth were divided into two separate worlds.

By the middle of the 15th century, Europeans were ready to expand their awareness of the world. Improvements in ships and navigation made it possible. They were spurred on by the hope of more trade with China, Japan, India, and the islands of Southeast Asia, called the Indies. Portuguese explorers were preparing to sail around Africa to reach India. But it was a long and difficult voyage. Many Europeans were looking for other routes.

Columbus's Voyages

Calculating the Distance A Genoese navigator, Christopher Columbus, said that a better way would be to sail west. Because the world was round, Columbus argued, the ships would eventually reach China and Japan.

Columbus was not alone in believing that the world was round. Many learned people agreed. But they differed with Columbus on how large the world was and how long it would take to reach the East. Columbus said the distance was only 2,400 miles. He was wrong—but his mistake was Spain's good fortune.

Columbus's First Voyage Columbus needed money and supplies to test his theory. He sought help in the courts of many European kings. Portugal, England, and France refused to finance the voyage. Finally, King Ferdinand and Queen Isabella of Spain gave him three ships—the *Niña,* the *Pinta,* and the *Santa María*—and a crew of 90 sailors. Columbus sailed from Spain on August 3, 1492.

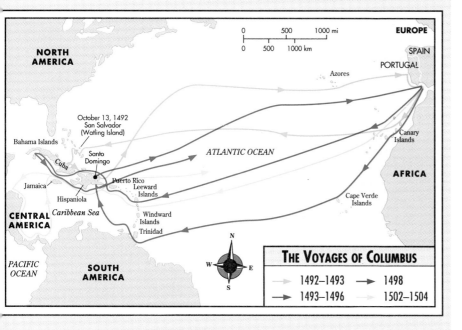

NORTH AMERICA

0 500 1000 mi
0 500 1000 km

EUROPE

SPAIN

PORTUGAL

Azores

October 13, 1492
San Salvador
(Watling Island)

Bahama Islands

ATLANTIC OCEAN

Canary
Islands

Santo
Domingo

Cuba

AFRICA

Jamaica

Puerto Rico
Leeward
Islands

Hispaniola

Cape Verde
Islands

CENTRAL AMERICA *Caribbean Sea*

Windward
Islands

Trinidad

N
W   E
S

PACIFIC OCEAN

SOUTH AMERICA

THE VOYAGES OF COLUMBUS	
1492–1493	1498
1493–1496	1502–1504

Even after his fourth voyage, Columbus remained convinced that he had reached Japan. The Americas were named after Amerigo Vespucci, the Italian navigator who was the first to recognize that Columbus had found two previously unknown continents.

Columbus stopped at the Canary Islands, where he spent some time refitting the ships. Finally, on September 6, the ships put out for their voyage of discovery. Three days later, the crew had its last sight of familiar land. A vast ocean stretched ahead.

As time passed, the sailors got worried because the voyage seemed too long. There were several sightings of land, but all proved false. Then, in a few days, the world changed:

- October 10: By now, the sailors were restless. Columbus promised that if land were not sighted in three days he would turn back.

- October 12: At 2:00 in the morning, Columbus got the news he wanted. A lookout perched atop the mast spotted land.

- October 13: Columbus stepped ashore, claiming that spot and all land around it for Spain.

Exploring the "Indies" No one knows exactly where Columbus landed. Most historians agree that it was somewhere in the Bahama Islands. Sure that he had reached the East, however, Columbus called the land the Indies and the people he met Indians.

Columbus spent the next few weeks exploring further. He left a small settlement of 40 men on the island of Hispaniola (the island now shared by Haiti and the Dominican Republic). The *Santa María* was wrecked off that island, and Columbus returned to Spain with his two remaining ships to a triumphant welcome.

Further Voyages Columbus made three more voyages, exploring many islands of the Caribbean and parts of the Central American coast. In his second voyage, he planted another settlement on Hispaniola. Now called Santo Domingo and the capital of the Dominican Republic, it is the oldest continuous European settlement in the Americas.

Columbus remained convinced that he had found a route to the East. Others soon realized that his real achievement was to bring Europe to the edge of a new world.

Effects of Uniting the World

The news that Columbus had reached the Indies changed Europe. Spain and many other countries mounted voyages of exploration. Within 50 years, the "Indians" of the New World and the Europeans of the Old World were swept up in a monumental meeting of cultures. The results of five centuries of contact were dramatic:

- Native Americans suffered. Their land was taken, and millions were killed by smallpox and other diseases brought from the Old World.

- As the Native Americans died out, Europeans brought African slaves to work in the Americas. African culture put its stamp on the new society.

- Europeans emigrated by the tens of millions to live in the Americas, creating new nations.

- The gold and silver that Spain took from the New World made it a great power. England, France, and Portugal soon joined the scramble to seize land and start colonies.

- Crops, such as corn, potatoes, and beans, were introduced from the New World to the Old.

- Horses, cattle, and pigs were brought from the Old World to the New, which had none.

Vasco da Gama

Da Gama was the first European to sail to India.

An excellent navigator who led his small fleet on a two-year journey into the unknown, da Gama was also cruel, brutally punishing those he saw as enemies.

The vessel being built in this print—a caravel—was one of the major improvements in ship design, enabling Europeans to safely undertake the long ocean voyages needed in the 15th and 16th centuries.

Seafaring People

In the late 15th century, Europe was poised to begin a great age of exploration. Europeans wanted to trade with China, Japan, and India without relying on the Muslim-controlled Silk Road through central Asia. To do so, they had to reach Asia by sea. Advances in shipbuilding and navigation enabled 15th-century Europeans to sail farther than before. But no one knew a sea route to Asia.

Portugal was one of the nations ready to try to find such a route. Throughout the 15th century, Portuguese navigators explored farther and farther along the West African coast. Then, in 1488, Bartholomeu Dias reached the southern tip of Africa and sailed into the Indian Ocean. Dias did not reach India, but his voyage gave the Portuguese what they wanted—a sea route to the East.

Da Gama's Voyage

The next step was to mount a major expedition to reach India itself and capture a share of its trade. The Portuguese king put a fleet of four ships under the command of Vasco da Gama, an able sailor and a ruthless man. On July 8, 1497, the ships left Lisbon.

The Voyage Out Da Gama's fleet swung into the western Atlantic. There the ships picked up currents and winds that carried them to southern Africa—a technique used by sailing ships to this day. This portion of the voyage kept the fleet out of sight of land for over three months, an unusually long period of time for that era. They finally rounded what is now called the Cape of Good Hope on November 22. On Christmas Day the fleet landed at the site of the present port of Durban on the East African coast. Da Gama named the area Natal

Europeans desired spices from the East to preserve and flavor foods—which was especially important in an age without refrigeration.

(Portuguese for "Christmas"), a name that the region still carries.

Da Gama also touched land in Mozambique, which he claimed for Portugal. At the thriving Muslim trading city of Moçambique, da Gama and his men pretended to be Muslims to ensure their safety. When this deceit was revealed, they were ordered to leave.

The Portuguese landed again farther north at Mombasa, a lively port in what is today Kenya. Suspicious of the warm welcome he had received, da Gama tortured four captives into confessing that an attack was coming. The Portuguese beat off the attack that night and then sailed on.

Next stop was Malindi, another port in modern Kenya. There da Gama used threats to get a pilot who knew the route to India. His ships crossed the Indian Ocean in 23 days, reaching Calicut on May 20, 1498.

Da Gama failed to negotiate a trade treaty with the local Hindu ruler for three reasons:

- The goods he had brought—cloth, hats, coral, and honey—were unappealing to the Indians, who wanted more valuable items.

- Da Gama claimed to have a large, powerful fleet, but Muslim merchants exposed the claim as a lie.

- News of the Portuguese sailors' bad behavior in Africa had reached Calicut.

Still, da Gama was able to trade for some spices. When tension between the Indians and the Portuguese rose, he left with his cargo for the return trip home.

The Passage Home The return trip was difficult. Poor winds delayed passage, and many of the crew died of scurvy, a disease that was common on long sea voyages. So many sailors were lost that one ship had to be burned for lack of a crew. The remaining ships became separated in a storm off West Africa. Eventually, on September 9, 1499—more than two years after leaving Africa—da Gama reached Lisbon. Two-thirds of his men (including his own brother) had died, mostly from scurvy.

Despite the losses, the trip was a triumph of navigation. Da Gama's leadership had guided his crew through dangerous and uncharted waters. Moreover, his cargo of spices was profitable.

The Aftermath

Da Gama made two other voyages to India, still using brutal force. At one point, he seized the cargo of a Muslim merchant ship and then burned the ship. By this act, he knowingly killed the ship's several hundred passengers, which included women and children. At one city in India, he killed captives to demonstrate Portuguese power.

Da Gama's voyage helped propel Portugal into a new status as a world trading power. Using guns and threats, the Portuguese wrested a share of the rich trade in spices from the Muslims, who had controlled it for centuries. By creating trading bases and colonies in India, Africa, and Brazil, the tiny European nation grew rich. Da Gama's voyage, along with that of Columbus, helped launch a long era of European colonialism in Asia, Africa, and the Americas.

9

Vasco Nuñez de Balboa

Spanish explorer Balboa was the first European to see the Pacific Ocean.

Settling the New World

Shortly after Christopher Columbus's epic first voyage, Europeans moved quickly to seize and conquer the new lands in the Americas. Within 20 years, the Spanish had started colonies in Cuba, Hispaniola, and other Caribbean islands and in parts of northern South America. Those colonies were settled by adventurers and the younger sons of nobles. Not content with lives as farmers, they sought gold and riches.

Among those adventurers was Vasco Nuñez de Balboa. His early life is obscure, but it is known that he first traveled to the New World in 1501. On that journey, his ship passed near Panama, where Balboa saw the Indian village called Darien. That encounter would shape his life.

First he settled in Hispaniola as a farmer but failed miserably. In 1510, to escape a mountain of debt, Balboa hid himself and his dog in a large barrel about to be loaded onto a ship. In this curious way, Balboa changed careers.

Balboa's ambition and vision helped lead him to the Pacific but—through conflict with Spanish authorities—also cost him his life.

The Discovery of the Pacific

Darien The ship, commanded by Martin Fernandez de Enciso, was taking supplies to a Spanish colony in present-day Colombia. Balboa revealed himself after the ship left port. While Enciso took a dislike to the stowaway, Balboa won the favor of the crew.

On its way to Colombia, the ship was met by another vessel coming from that colony. The commander of that ship, Francisco Pizarro, reported that Indian attacks and disease had killed all the colonists except those on the ship. Enciso decided to continue regardless, and Pizarro returned with him. But as the ships neared the colony, Enciso accidentally ran aground. Pizarro took Enciso's crew aboard, and all debated what to do next.

Balboa then suggested that they sail to Darien, which he remembered from his earlier voyage. The others agreed.

Arriving at Darien, Balboa established a settlement. Seeing a chance to remove an enemy, he ousted Enciso from command and shipped him back to Spain. Balboa was chosen as governor by the men at Darien.

Balboa now had free rein, and in two years of rule he amassed a large fortune. From the Indians he heard of a "great water" to the west (the Pacific Ocean). They also told him of a land of vast wealth called Biru (Peru) to the south. He resolved to find this land full of gold.

Driven by their desire for gold, silver, and jewelry such as these Native American ear ornaments, the Spanish conquered much of Central and South America.

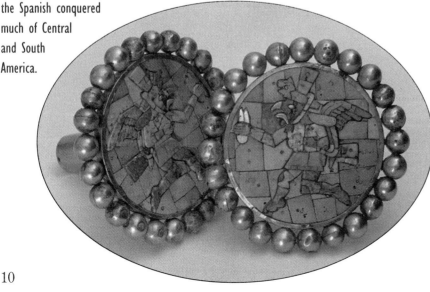

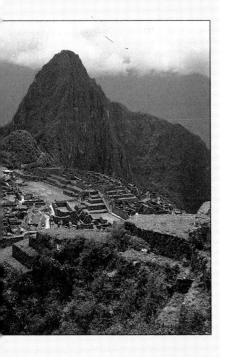

The remains of the rich Inca civilization can be seen at these ruins in Machu Picchu, in the Andes Mountains. Similar ruins are all that remain of the great Native American civilizations of Mexico.

The Expedition

On September 1, 1513, Balboa led 190 Spaniards and 800 Native Americans on an expedition to find the western sea. Pizarro was one of his lieutenants. Fortunately they were crossing where the Isthmus of Panama was narrowest. Balboa befriended the first Indian chief he met and was given some native guides to lead him west.

The Spaniards made slow progress through the jungle. They suffered in their armor from the hot weather and dense growth. At another Indian village, they learned of a ridge from which the ocean could be seen. But it took four days to trek the 30 miles to that site. Once they reached the ridge, Balboa mounted it alone, becoming the first European to see the Pacific Ocean. He named it the South Sea and claimed the ocean, its islands, and all surrounding lands for Spain.

The Conquest of America

Balboa's Later Career Laden with riches they had taken from Indians, Balboa and his men barely made it back to Darien. In the meantime, his situation had changed. His old enemy Enciso had described Balboa's behavior to the Spanish king, who sent another governor to Darien. Once back, Balboa found himself in a struggle for power with that governor.

Balboa pursued his plans to explore more of the Pacific coast. He built two ships on that coast—having used Indian slaves, many of whom died, to carry the materials overland. After a failed attempt to sail south, Balboa was met by Pizarro, now serving the new governor. Pizarro arrested Balboa for disobeying the governor's orders and took him back to Darien. There he was tried for treason, convicted, and quickly beheaded.

Conquest of the Native Americans Balboa's settlement at Darien firmly positioned the Spanish on the Central American mainland. From that base, they conquered the rich Indian nations there.

In 1517, Hernández de Córdoba discovered the Yucatán Peninsula of present-day Mexico. There he saw the remains of the great Maya civilization, which had perished two hundred years earlier. He also heard stories of an even richer land in the interior.

In 1519, Hernando Cortés set out to find that land and subdue its people. He marched inland and reached the beautiful capital of the Aztecs, Tenochtitlán (on the site of present-day Mexico City). Cortés seized the ruler, Moctezuma. When troubles arose, Cortés was forced to fight his way out of the city. But the Aztecs were doomed. A smallpox epidemic swept their land. This disease, common in Europe, had never appeared in the Americas before. It killed as many as three and a half million Aztecs in less than a year. The Spanish went on to completely occupy Central America.

The other great Spanish conquest was achieved by Balboa's old associate Pizarro, who sought the rumored land of Biru. In 1532, on his third attempt, he finally reached the center of the Inca Empire in the Andes Mountains. Weakened by disease and civil war, the Incas fell quickly to Pizarro's force, though it was small. With this conquest, the Spanish began possession of much of South America.

> Is it possible that you should value so much a thing that so little deserves your esteem? And that you should leave the repose of your houses, and pass so many seas, exposed to such dangers, to trouble those who live quiet in their own country? Have some shame, Christians—do not value these things; but, if you are resolved to search for gold, I will show you a country where you may satisfy yourselves.
>
> —spoken by an Indian to Balboa

Ferdinand Magellan

〜

A Portuguese navigator, Magellan, led the first expedition that sailed completely around the world.

Magellan's seamanship and leadership ability were important in achieving one of the great navigational feats of history—the first circumnavigation of the world. His expedition linked Europe and Asia by way of the Pacific Ocean and opened the door to a new world of trade and exploration.

Rival Powers

Around the turn of the 16th century, Spain and Portugal became rivals for the new trade routes discovered by voyages of exploration. Portugal controlled the route around Africa. Christopher Columbus, sailing for Spain, had found a new world. Spain was pleased but still wanted to reach Asia by sailing west.

A Portuguese navigator, Ferdinand Magellan, believed that such a route was possible. He tried to get the king of Portugal to back a western expedition. But the king wasn't interested. So Magellan went to King Charles of Spain. His plan was simple. He would sail south along the coast of South America until he reached the tip of the landmass or a passage west. Then he would head west to the sea that Balboa had called the South Sea (the Pacific Ocean) and continue sailing until he reached Asia. Charles agreed to finance the trip.

Around the World

Magellan was about 40 years old. He had helped build the growing Portuguese trading empire in India and had fought in a number of battles there. He had sailed east from India to the Moluccas, then called the Spice Islands, and may even have gone as far as the Philippines. Brave and skilled at navigation, he was an excellent leader for the daring expedition.

He left Spain with five ships on September 20, 1519. The voyage did not begin well. A Spaniard commanding one of the five ships challenged Magellan, hoping to kill the leader and take command himself. Magellan overcame the mutiny and imprisoned his challenger. Storms followed by calm seas hampered the fleet's passage across the Atlantic. Still, the ships reached Brazil by December 8.

Sailing down the Atlantic coast of South America, the fleet reached a huge expanse of water opening to the west. Hoping it was a way to Balboa's ocean, Magellan sent a ship to investigate. In fact, he had found the broad

estuary of the Río de la Plata (in modern Argentina and Uruguay) and had to continue farther south.

The fleet spent much of 1520 repairing the ships. In that time, Magellan faced many hardships.

- He had to quell another mutiny.

- He found that he had been given only half the stores of food he had been promised.

- One of the ships ran aground and had to be abandoned.

In mid-October 1520, the fleet set sail again. Later that month, they passed below the southern tip of South America. One ship became separated from the others and returned to Spain. The remaining three ships sailed through the dangerous strait between the South American continent and Tierra del Fuego. That strait was later named the Strait of Magellan in honor of the navigator. The passage took 37 days. On reaching the open sea, which was calm, Magellan gave it the name used for it today, the Pacific ("peaceful") Ocean.

Magellan hoped to reach the Spice Islands in four weeks, but the voyage dragged on. Food ran out or rotted. Sailors were reduced to eating sawdust, oxhide, and rats. They mixed seawater with fresh for something to drink. Many died of scurvy.

After stopping briefly at two uninhabited islands, the fleet finally touched land at Guam. They had been sailing in the Pacific for over four months. By mid-March 1521 they reached the Philippine Islands. Magellan had sailed east to the Indies earlier in his career. Now he had reached them by sailing west. He was, in effect, the first person to sail around the world. But this particular voyage was about to end for him.

Magellan enjoyed good relations with some Filipinos. But a disagreement arose with one group. When a fight resulted, Magellan was killed. He died fighting on shore to allow his men to escape to the ship. The chronicler of the expedition noted sadly, "And so they slew our mirror, our light, our comfort and our true and only guide."

The Return to Spain

The new commander of the fleet burned one of the ships and led the sailors into piracy. After a few months of piracy, Juan Sebastián de Elcano was given command. He led the ships to the Spice Islands in November 1521. Leaving one ship for repairs, he sailed the *Victoria,* Magellan's flagship, back to Spain. He had only 49 of the original crew of about 250.

Elcano reached Spain on September 8, 1522—more than three years after Magellan had left that land. Only 18 of the original crew remained alive. The first voyage to sail around the world was finally complete.

Though Magellan himself did not survive, his voyage was a triumph of navigation. He proved what Columbus had said—that one could reach the East by sailing west. He found the passage—the strait that bears his name—to reach the Pacific from the Atlantic. And he opened the vast stretches of the Pacific Ocean to further exploration.

◄ Magellan's crew, passing through the narrow strait named after the navigator, were the first Europeans to see the southern tip of South America.

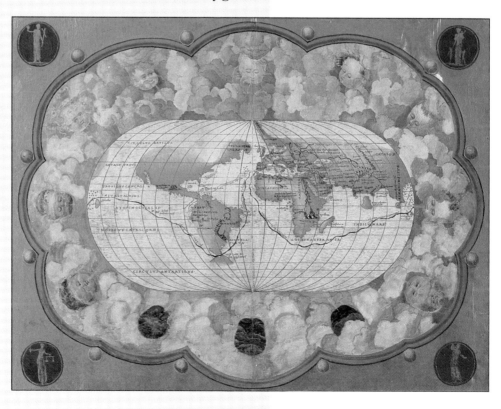

► This map of the world, painted in 1543 (about 20 years after Magellan's voyage) shows the route of the Magellan expedition—and how Europeans viewed the world at the time.

Francisco Vasquez de Coronado

The journey of Coronado added a vast area of what is now the southwestern United States to the Spanish Empire.

The Search for Gold

By the 1530s, warfare and disease had helped the Spanish conquer the Aztec Empire of Mexico and the Inca Empire of South America. These conquests brought Spain large amounts of gold and silver. Wherever they turned, it seemed, the Spanish found precious metals. And so when they heard rumors of the Seven Cities of Gold in Cíbola, in the region north of Mexico, they resolved to find—and conquer—them.

In 1539, a monk named Marcos de Niza led a small party to find these cities. In the group was an African slave named Esteban, who had been part of an earlier expedition. At one point, Esteban was sent to scout ahead. Mistaking the sunlight shining on pueblos (dwellings made of stone or brick) and cornfields of the Zuni Indians for gold, he sent word back that he had found the cities. When Esteban was killed by Indians, de Niza turned back to Mexico. But he reported that he had located Cíbola.

Coronado's Great Trek

The Search for Cíbola De Niza made his report to Francisco Vasquez de Coronado, governor of a region of New Spain (part of present-day Mexico). Coronado secured the command of a major expedition to find the cities. He then assembled a party of 340 Spaniards, 300 Mexican Indians, and about 1,000 Indian and African slaves. They set out in late February 1540, bringing along herds of livestock for food. De Niza was a guide.

The party marched up the coast of western Mexico, then headed north to cross into present-day Arizona. They finally turned east and entered modern New Mexico, where, in July, de Niza showed them what he thought was Cíbola.

What they found was no golden city, but one of the six pueblos of the Zuni Indians. These cliff houses were impressive structures, but they did not contain riches. The Spanish attacked and seized the pueblos anyway.

In the following months, Coronado sent out parties to explore the other Zuni pueblos and some Hopi Indian villages farther north. Another party found the Colorado River and became the first Europeans to behold the Grand Canyon.

The Spaniards were disappointed by the lack of wealth. As they wintered in 1540–1541, they were also troubled by bad weather and constant Indian attacks. But then they heard from an Indian named "the Turk" of another city of gold, belonging to the Quivira tribe, far to the north. Coronado resolved to find this site of riches.

The March to the Quivira Coronado left for his new destination in late April 1541. As the party crossed into

Coronado's route took him through the modern states of Arizona, New Mexico, Texas, Oklahoma, and Kansas. This trek forged a Spanish claim to what would later be the southwestern United States.

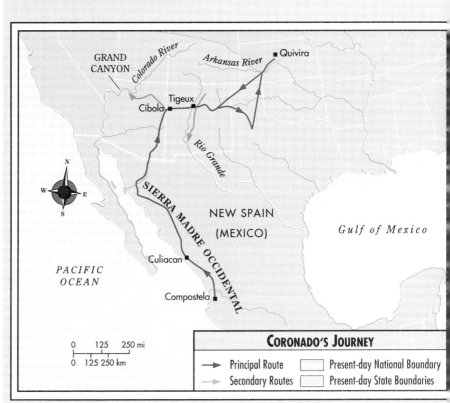

present-day Texas, they saw part of the vast prairie that marks the Great Plains. They also encountered herds of "humpbacked oxen"—bison.

After the party spent five weeks marching seemingly aimlessly in the area, Coronado confronted the Turk, who admitted that he had no idea where the Quivira lived. Coronado had the Turk killed, sent the main body of his party back to its base, and took a smaller group due north, following the advice of local Indians.

They marched north for over a month, reaching what is now central Kansas. There they found a village of the Quivira Indians (later called Wichita Indians)—but no gold. Coronado explored farther for a little while, but he had given up hope. His party, helped by the Quivira, returned to its base.

After wintering there, he led his expedition back to Mexico in the spring of 1542. Having found no gold, Coronado felt he had failed. A member of the expedition described him as "very sad and very weary, completely worn out and shamefaced."

The Spanish Southwest

While Coronado found no gold, he opened vast new reaches of land to the growing Spanish empire in the Americas. The Spanish settled in what is now Texas, New Mexico, Arizona, and California. In those areas they created thriving communities, which were held by Spain, and then Mexico, for about 300 years.

Many reminders of centuries of Spanish control are still seen:

- Such cities as Los Angeles, San Diego, and San Francisco grew up around missions that the Spanish founded.
- Many topographical features, such as the Rio Grande ("large river") and Sierra Nevada ("snowy mountains"), have Spanish names.
- Many people of these states celebrate their Spanish heritage on festival days.

Coronado may not have found gold, but his journey left its stamp on American history.

This church in Tucson reflects the Spanish colonial style found throughout the Southwest.

Weary from two years of traveling through the hot Southwest and despondent over finding no gold, Coronado headed back to New Spain.

Jacques Cartier

Cartier was the first European to find the St. Lawrence River, the main route into northern North America.

With the Spanish finding gold and silver in Central and South America, the French king sent Jacques Cartier to find wealth in North America.

The wooden fort in this French painting from 1547 suggests that relations between the French and the Native Americans were not always smooth.

Rivals in the New World

Spurred on by news of the voyages of Christopher Columbus and Vasco da Gama, the Spanish and Portuguese raced to build empires. With the conquest of Mexico, the Spanish got a foothold on the American mainland to add to their island holdings. The Portuguese began to settle Brazil. But in the early 1500s, the potential of the Americas was still not fully realized. The goal was still to find a quick way to reach Asia, which offered wealth from trade.

The English and French jumped into this competition as well:

- Italian navigators John Cabot and his son Sebastian sailed for the English, exploring the eastern edges of what would become Canada.

- Another Italian, Giovanni da Verrazano, explored along the Atlantic coast of North America for France.

Their goal was to find the Northwest Passage—an open sea lane from the Atlantic to the Pacific that everyone believed must exist.

Cartier's Voyages

The king of France, Francis I, chose Jacques Cartier to undertake his kingdom's next major effort to find the Northwest Passage. Cartier was an experienced sailor who may have journeyed with Verrazano.

The First Voyage Cartier left France in April 1534 with two ships and 61 men. He crossed the Atlantic in only 20 days, reaching Newfoundland on May 10. He explored around Newfoundland and the Gulf of St. Lawrence, spotting Prince Edward Island and parts of the New Brunswick shore.

Landing on the Gaspé Peninsula, Cartier claimed the land for France. There Cartier met Indians led by a chief named Donnaconna. They were a fishing party from a large village at the present site of the city of Quebec. The two leaders agreed that two of Donnaconna's sons would return with Cartier to Europe. In July, Cartier set out for home.

The Second Voyage Received as a hero, Cartier set out again in 1535 with three ships and 110 men. After a difficult crossing, Donnaconna's sons led Cartier right to the St. Lawrence River, which the French explorer was convinced was the Northwest Passage. Shortly after entering the river, they spotted a large feeder river coming from the north. The Indians told Cartier that this river flowed from Saguenay, a wealthy kingdom. Cartier took note but continued to sail west.

He reached Donnaconna's village and continued on to another Indian village at present-day Montreal. Cartier named the height that overlooked that site Mont Real ("Royal Mountain").

Cartier was unable to continue west—rapids just beyond the mountain prevented his ships from sailing any farther. He and his crew spent a miserable winter. The cold was severe, food supplies were low, and the entire crew suffered from scurvy. About a quarter of the crew died.

Cartier determined to return to France in the spring. A new goal was taking shape: to find the rich kingdom of Saguenay. To convince his king to support this plan, he kidnapped Donnaconna and took him back to France.

The Third Voyage The king agreed that finding Saguenay was a worthy goal, but a war with Spain delayed the expedition. In 1541, Cartier finally left with five ships and one thousand colonists.

The trip was a failure. It began by establishing a settlement near the site of modern Quebec. But Cartier's various attempts to find Saguenay failed. They had to, because no such kingdom existed. The colonists then suffered a difficult winter, plagued by scurvy and attacks by Native Americans.

In the spring, Cartier decided to abandon the settlement. The minerals that the French brought back were worthless. What they thought were diamonds and gold turned out to be only quartz and iron pyrite—"fool's gold."

From New France to Quebec

Cartier's mission may have failed, but his voyages had a major impact on the history of North America. By exploring the area along the St. Lawrence, he staked a French claim to this region. It took many decades for France to take advantage of this foothold. Still, by the middle of the 17th century there were French settlements all along the river and in the eastern Great Lakes. The area was called New France.

Though the English chased the French from that territory in 1763, the Quebec of today is Cartier's legacy. Citizens of the Canadian province of Quebec are fiercely proud of their French heritage. French is the province's official language, and French customs color its everyday life. The desire of French Canadians to maintain their identity has created political tension in Canada, a largely English-speaking nation. That tension is yet to be resolved.

This plaza in the old French section of Montreal is named for Cartier, an enduring legacy of the French settlement of Canada.

Henry Hudson

Hudson tried to locate a waterway north of America to sail to Asia and established a Dutch claim to land in North America.

Passage to the East

From the middle of the 15th century to the middle of the 17th, most explorers had a similar goal. They wanted to find a water route from Europe to Asia. The Spanish and Portuguese came to control the southern routes around Africa and South America. The English tried to find a northern route. One such route, called the Northwest Passage, was supposed to lead north of North America. The other, the Northeast Passage, supposedly went north of Russia.

A number of explorers looked for the Northwest Passage:

- John Cabot, an Italian sailing for England, landed on what is today Nova Scotia.

- Martin Frobisher and John Davis explored the icy waters north of eastern Canada.

- Sir Francis Drake sailed around South America and then up the Pacific coast of North America to find where the passage had its outlet.

Others tried the Northeast route, which the Dutch were also interested in. By the early 1600s, though, all attempts had failed.

The Voyages of Hudson

Henry Hudson was another English explorer who attempted to find an easy route to Asia. His first two voyages were aimed at the Northeast Passage. Undertaken for an English merchant company, they succeeded in locating rich waters for whaling near what is today called Spitsbergen in the Arctic Ocean near Norway. But they found no passage to Asia.

One for the Dutch In 1609, Hudson was at sea again, but this time for the Dutch. Hudson was told to take his ship, the *Half Moon,* either east or west—the Dutch didn't care. Hudson first tried the eastern route one more time. But after a month of sailing, ice and fog made the navigation difficult. The crew—only about 20 men—was growing restless. They wanted to turn back. When Hudson

As the ship sailed up the river named for Hudson, the crew put ashore from time to time to trade with Native Americans.

Although he was a fine navigator, Hudson's inability to control his crew led to his death on his final voyage of exploration.

offered them the option of trying the Northwest Passage, they seized the chance to leave the icy waters.

Hudson guided the ship west and touched a number of points in the present United States. He sailed past Cape Cod and explored the Chesapeake and Delaware bays. He entered New York Bay, which had already been found by Verrazano. Then Hudson sailed up the river that flows west of present-day Manhattan Island. He traveled north, almost to modern Albany, when the crew's renewed restlessness forced him to turn back. In his honor, the river was later named for him.

This was Hudson's first and only voyage for the Dutch. On his return trip to Holland, he stopped in England. There he was seized by English officials. If he sailed again, they said, it would be for England.

Hudson's Last Voyage Sail for England he did. The next year, 1610, Hudson set out again to find the Northwest Passage. This time he resolved to look farther north. He entered Hudson Strait, between Baffin Island and Newfoundland. In August he entered the huge bay in northern Canada that now bears his name.

The vast expanse of water probably made Hudson think that he had reached his goal—it had to be a way to Asia. Then the ship reached James Bay, at the southern end of Hudson Bay. Growing discouraged, Hudson spent some weeks crossing and recrossing that bay. The crew wondered about his sanity. When the ship's mate, speaking for the crew, expressed their fears, Hudson tried him for mutiny and replaced him. The crew's mood worsened; tensions rose.

In November, Hudson beached the ship, which was then frozen in by ice. The crew spent a very difficult winter, suffering from scurvy and hunger.

When the ship finally set sail again in June, Hudson announced his intention to look again for the Northwest Passage. The crew, knowing that only two weeks' worth of food remained, could take no more. They put Hudson, his son, and six others in a small boat with a few supplies and then cast them adrift. They sailed on to England, leaving Hudson and his party to certain death.

New Amsterdam

Hudson, like all who came before or after seeking the Northwest Passage, failed in his main goal. But his third voyage had a lasting effect.

Intrigued by his voyage up what is now called the Hudson River, the Dutch came to settle that area of North America. They bought the island that the Indians called Mannahatta. And on that island—today called Manhattan—they built the settlement of New Amsterdam.

From their base in New Amsterdam, the Dutch built other settlements up the Hudson River and westward along the Mohawk River. They held this region until 1664, when they were forced to surrender it to the English. Then New Amsterdam got its present name—New York.

But the Dutch heritage in New York lives on. Dutch place-names dot the eastern parts of the state. And three presidents—Martin Van Buren and both Roosevelts—had Dutch ancestry.

The Hudson River today remains a beautiful stretch of water dotted by many communities that still bear the names created by the Dutch settlers who came after Henry Hudson.

Louis Jolliet and Jacques Marquette

Explorer Jolliet and priest Marquette explored the upper reaches of the Mississippi River.

Marquette (standing) and Jolliet (seated behind him) enjoyed good relations with the Native Americans they met on their travels.

New France

The French were slow to exploit the foothold in North America that Jacques Cartier gave them in the 16th century. Wars against Spain delayed any major colonizing effort for many decades. By the beginning of the 17th century, though, Samuel de Champlain established permanent settlements at Quebec and Montreal. He explored the area along the St. Lawrence and the eastern Great Lakes. When he himself could not explore, he sent others to do so. New France was growing.

Champlain helped this growth with a decision. To pass the many rapids and small rivers, he decided, the French must use the tools of the Indians. And so it was with light, easily portable canoes that the region was explored by *voyageurs*. (French for "traveler"; a *voyageur* was a backwoods guide and fur trader.)

Furs and Bibles

Unable to mine gold or silver, as the Spanish were doing farther south, the French found other riches in their colonies. They exchanged furs for guns, tobacco, and wampum (beads used by Native Americans as money). The furs were then shipped back to Europe and sold at a profit. To find new sources of pelts, the *voyageurs* plunged deeper into the North American wilderness.

Another set of adventurers was also expanding French knowledge of the area. Jesuit missionaries canoed into new regions. Their aim was to convert the Native Americans to Christianity. Both missionaries and traders reported to French officials on what they had learned.

"Big Water"

Among those reports were tales of a great river to the west of the Great Lakes. The governor of New France wondered where it led. Did it flow to the south, to the Gulf of Mexico and Spanish lands? Or could it be the waterway that every European nation wanted, the Northwest Passage to Asia? He decided to send someone to find out.

Down the Mississippi

Louis Jolliet was chosen as the expedition's chief. Jolliet, born in New France, became the first North American native of European descent to explore areas of the continent. He chose his friend Jacques Marquette, a Jesuit priest who knew six Indian languages, to accompany him.

The two spent the winter of 1672–1673 talking to Indians and planning their route. They ignored warnings about fierce tribes and vicious monsters. On May 17, 1673, they left the Straits of Mackinac (which separate upper and lower Michigan) with five *voyageurs* in two canoes.

The party made rapid progress. They paddled west on Lake Michigan to Green Bay, where they entered the Fox River. From the Fox they portaged, or carried their canoes, to the Wisconsin River. They paddled down the Wisconsin to the Mississippi, reaching that river a month after starting out.

After another month of travel, all on the Mississippi, they stopped.

Having reached the spot where the Arkansas River enters the Mississippi, they now knew that this river was not the Northwest Passage. Both noted the size of the Missouri River, which entered the Mississippi from the west, and wondered whether the Missouri was that much-sought route. They were sure that the Mississippi flowed south, and Indians told them that they were only ten days from its mouth. They were also sure that the Spanish held the lower reaches of the river; Spanish goods had been found in Indian hands, undoubtedly the result of trade.

The party had made remarkable progress, having traveled 2,500 miles by canoe in four months. They returned by a slightly different route, slowed by the need to paddle upriver. Marquette stopped to rest in Green Bay. Jolliet returned to Montreal. Unfortunately, his canoe overturned in rapids just outside that city. He survived the spill, but his map and notes were lost.

The Mississippi, the largest river of North America, became a key to French holdings in what is now the United States. The section of the river shown here is in northeast Iowa.

A Larger New France

Although Jolliet's papers were lost, a journal that may have been written by Marquette survives. (Historians are unsure whether the Jesuit actually wrote it or whether it was compiled by someone else from Marquette's recollections.) That journal described some of the new animals that the French saw, such as catfish and bison. It told of the calumet, or peace pipe, that the party was given by one group of Native Americans. And it explained the mystery of the monsters that the Indians had warned them of. They were large paintings on the cliffs lining the river bank, left by artists from other Indian tribes.

Jolliet and Marquette's journey had settled the main issue for the French: the Mississippi was not the Northwest Passage. Within a few years, another expedition set out. René-Robert Cavelier, Sieur de La Salle, explored the length of the Mississippi to its source. This trip led to the addition of large areas of land to New France and a lasting French stamp on the Mississippi valley.

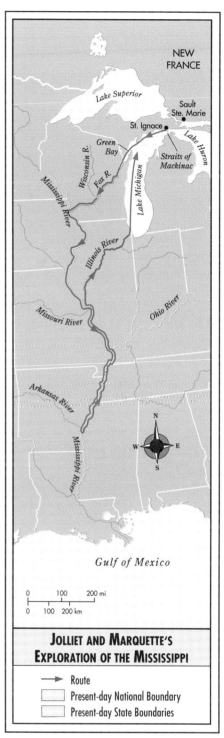

JOLLIET AND MARQUETTE'S EXPLORATION OF THE MISSISSIPPI

→ Route
☐ Present-day National Boundary
☐ Present-day State Boundaries

Jolliet and Marquette began their great journey at the Jesuit mission of St. Ignace, near the Straits of Mackinac. Their voyage proved that the Mississippi was not the long-sought Northwest Passage.

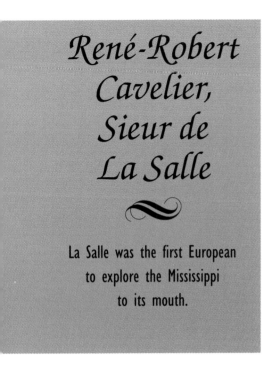

René-Robert Cavelier, Sieur de La Salle

La Salle was the first European to explore the Mississippi to its mouth.

The son of a wealthy merchant, La Salle was a bold adventurer more suited to exploration than to the priesthood, his first calling.

Ambition and Goals

René-Robert Cavelier—better known by his title, Sieur de La Salle—was a daring and ambitious man. He studied to become a Jesuit priest but soon abandoned that calling for a life of adventure.

He first tried farming in New France, the French colony in North America. After three years he abandoned that career as well. In 1669, he began his true vocation: exploring.

By 1672, La Salle was commanding a French trading post on Lake Ontario. There he heard of the voyage of Louis Jolliet and Jacques Marquette down the Mississippi. He formed a plan to explore that great river farther and build French forts along its length. His goal was to expand the size of French holdings in North America and contain the British, who were settling on the Atlantic Coast. La Salle told his plan to the governor of New France, who sent him to France to present his plan to the king.

La Salle's Expeditions

Down the Mississippi King Louis XIV approved La Salle's plan to explore and establish forts. But the king refused to finance the voyage; La Salle would have to raise his own funds. He returned to New France in 1678 with Henri de Tonti, an Italian adventurer who would be his trusted companion for many years.

La Salle thought big. To raise the money for his trip, he determined to trade and sell furs. To amass a sizable load of furs, he built a ship called the *Griffin,* the first commercial ship to sail the Great Lakes. In the fall of 1679 he gathered furs in the areas around Lakes Erie, Huron, and Michigan, then sent the ship back to more settled areas. Unfortunately, it was never heard from again; it probably sank in a storm.

Painted many centuries after La Salle's voyage, this painting depicts him claiming Louisiana for France while his party—and curious Native Americans—look on.

Meanwhile, La Salle built Fort Miami where St. Joseph, Michigan, now stands. During the winter of 1679–1680 he and his party explored along the Kankakee and Illinois rivers, building another fort on the latter near the site of modern Peoria, Illinois. Anxious because he had no news of the *Griffin,* La Salle left Tonti in command of his party and trekked 1,000 miles overland back to New France. Learning of the ship's disappearance, La Salle managed to raise some money anyway. When he returned to the fort on the Illinois, however, he found it destroyed and his men gone.

La Salle returned again to New France to complete preparations for the voyage down the Mississippi. In June 1681, he was finally reunited with Tonti and his men. They had been captured by Indians, but escaped and found their way back to New France.

After two years of preparations, the party finally left for the Mississippi in December 1681. The voyage itself was fairly uneventful. By mid-March they reached the Arkansas River, where Jolliet and Marquette's expedition had stopped. When Indians approached, La Salle offered the calumet, or peace pipe, and his party was welcomed. La Salle claimed the Indians' land for France and soon set out again. By April 6, 1682, they had reached the river's mouth. On April 9, La Salle claimed the river and all the land around it for the king of France. He named the region Louisiana in the king's honor.

A Goal Not Reached La Salle wanted to build a fort near the river's mouth. When the governor of New France disapproved of the idea, La Salle set out for France to get the king's agreement. With that approval, he mounted a major expedition that left France in July 1684.

Unfortunately, the expedition failed in its goal. The ship sailed past the mouth of the Mississippi and landed the men in present-day Texas, near Galveston. After two unsuccessful attempts to march overland to the river, the men grew restless. Tired of wandering, they had lost confidence in La Salle. When a third attempt also failed, they killed him.

French North America

La Salle's life may have ended in failure, but he achieved one of his major goals: he laid the groundwork for a larger French empire in North America. Indeed, France was well positioned to dominate the continent. Unfortunately for La Salle, the king was uninterested in taking advantage of this position. He never fully developed the ring of forts that La Salle had advocated. In the middle of the 18th century, a lost war with England forced the French to give up New France. At the beginning of the 19th century, Napoleon's need for money forced the French to sell Louisiana to the United States.

Despite this inability to control the region, the French left their mark on the area. French names can be found from Detroit to St. Louis. The state of Louisiana bears the stamp of French influence. Its laws, for instance, are based on French, not English, law, and counties are designated as parishes.

Cartier, Jolliet and Marquette, and La Salle are but a few of the many French explorers of northern North America who helped extend the territory of New France.

FRENCH EXPLORERS IN NORTH AMERICA		
Explorer	**Main Years of Activity**	**Region Explored**
Samuel de Champlain	1603–1615	Eastern Canada
Etienne Brulé	1610–1632	Great Lakes
Jean Nicollet de Belleborne	1618–1635	Lake Michigan, Green Bay
Louis Hennepin	1676–1681	Upper Mississippi River
Daniel Greysolon, Sieur Dulhut	1678–1681, 1683–1686	Upper Great Lakes
Pierre le Moyne, Sieur d'Iberville	1698–1701	Lower Mississippi River
Pierre Charlevoix	1720–1722	Great Lakes, Mississippi River

Vitus Bering

Danish explorer Bering discovered that Asia is separated from North America by a narrow strait, now named for him.

The stormy and icy waters near Siberia and Alaska created a formidable challenge for Bering and his expedition.

The Rise of Russia

As the powers of western Europe expanded outward to new worlds in the mid-16th century, the Russian Empire was beginning to form as well. The Russian czars, or emperors, conquered neighboring lands. Over the next 100 years, bold adventurers explored stretches of Siberia, east of Russia. They found a cold, harsh land where the ground beneath the surface was permanently frozen.

These adventurers eventually reached the eastern edge of Siberia, including the peninsula called Kamchatka. When Peter the Great became czar, near the end of the 17th century, he wished to know exactly what lay to the east of Siberia. Was Asia connected to North America? Was there an easy route from Russia to China and Japan? To answer these questions, Peter hired a Danish sailor named Vitus Bering. This Dane made two great explorations of what came to be called Alaska. The second cost him his life.

Bering's Expeditions

Preparations Bering's trips were large expeditions that required long preparation. Starting from St. Petersburg, Russia, he had to—

- Trek thousands of miles across Siberia.
- Build a ship.
- Sail it to Kamchatka.
- Cross that peninsula.
- Build another ship, which was to be used for the actual exploring.

These preparations took three and a half years for his first trip and eight years for the second.

Bering's way would have been easier had he simply sailed around Europe, Africa, and Asia and north up the Asian coast. But Peter the Great wanted to hide his expeditions from other nations. He also wanted to impress the Siberians—fairly new subjects of the Russian throne—with his nation's might. So Bering had to take a more difficult way.

The First Voyage In July 1728, Bering set out from Kamchatka the first time. He headed northeast along the Siberian coast. By August, he had reached a small island at the end of the strait which now bears his name and which divides Asia and North America.

Here he hesitated. His instructions were to settle the question of whether Asia and America were linked. That meant sailing on. But he was concerned that a winter this far north would be hazardous. He explored northward for a few days but did not see the land of North America. Then he decided to turn back. When he reached St. Petersburg in March 1730, Bering suggested another trip.

The Second Voyage This so-called Great Northern Expedition began in 1733. It included 3,000 men; among them were painters, surveyors, and scientists to record and note what was found.

This is the Bering Strait as it looks today. The bleak and icy landscape has remained unchanged since Bering's exploration.

Russian Alaska, Spanish California

Though fatal to Bering, his expedition was a success for the Russians. The survivors returned with news of rich fur-hunting grounds in the Aleutians and Alaska. They told of seals, sea otters, and foxes. The Russians returned year after year to hunt for furs. As they explored Alaska farther, they laid claim to it—a claim that lasted until Russia sold Alaska to the United States in the 1860s.

Perhaps the most interesting result of Bering's voyages was its effect on the Spanish in Mexico. Worried about the Russians moving south down the Pacific Coast, the Spanish began an aggressive policy of settling California. They built a series of missions from San Diego up to San Francisco in this period. These missions became the basis of the Spanish culture of California—and of great modern cities. The Russians meanwhile did reach as far south as Fort Ross about 100 miles north of San Francisco.

By June 1741, Bering and his party were ready to sail from Kamchatka in two ships. He commanded the *St. Peter;* a Russian named Aleksei Chirikov captained the *St. Paul.* A storm separated the two ships. Bering sailed northeast, finally reaching the coast of present-day Alaska on July 18. His men went ashore on an island now called Kayak Island.

The *St. Peter* explored the islands south of Alaska, including Kodiak Island and the Aleutians. As the ship headed home, supplies dwindled. Many of the crew, including Bering, were stricken with scurvy. The weather and winds turned against the explorers as well. Headwinds slowed progress, and thick fogs made navigation difficult. The *St. Peter* was wrecked on the rocks of an island near Kamchatka.

The crew wintered on the island, now called Bering Island. It was a bleak land with no trees and little driftwood to make fires. For shelter, the men dug holes in which they huddled under sails for cover. By killing seals and sea otters, they got both food and clothing. But their suffering continued. Blue foxes harassed the men, chewed on the sailcloth, and stole food.

In the summer of 1742, the men rebuilt a ship from the wreckage of the *St. Peter* and sailed back to Kamchatka. There they rejoined Chirikov—he had returned the previous year. But the voyage home was made without Bering. He had died on the island about a month after the crew had landed.

Parkas like this one, made of 75 bird skins, were common in Alaska and the Aleutian Islands. Siberian parkas were usually made of caribou hides.

25

James Cook

ENGLISH CIRCUMNAVIGATORS BEFORE COOK		
Explorer	Duration of Voyage	Number of Ships
Sir Francis Drake	Dec. 13, 1577–Sept. 26, 1580	5 (2 returned)
Thomas Cavendish	July 21, 1586–Sept. 9, 1588	3 (1 returned)
George Anson	Sept. 18, 1740–June 15, 1744	6 (1 returned)
John Byron	June 21, 1764–May 9, 1766	2 (2 returned)
Samuel Wallis	Aug. 21, 1766–May 19, 1768	1 (1 returned)
Philip Carteret	Aug. 21, 1766–Mar. 20, 1769	1 (1 returned)

Cook's rise from farmer's son to captain in the Royal Navy was unusual, but he became the most noted English seaman of his time.

Cook was not the first English captain to command a voyage that circumnavigated the globe. But his three voyages yielded much valuable scientific information.

Scientific Exploration

In the 18th century, Europeans were still exploring the Americas and the Pacific, but their goals had changed. No longer were they searching for gold or spices. The object now was to gain knowledge. Great Britain backed such voyages of discovery, and its greatest discoverer was James Cook.

Cook rose from humble origins. The son of a farmer, he had little schooling. In his teens he joined a coal ship as a cabin boy. After nine years in the coal trade, he volunteered to be a seaman in the Royal Navy. (This was unusual; most sailors were pressed into the service, forced to join by gangs that prowled the wharves.) Cook rose through the ranks, finally obtaining his own command in 1764. Two years later, while conducting a sea survey off the east coast of Canada, he made notes on a solar eclipse. When these notes caught the eye of influential scientists, Cook's career as an explorer began. Through connections with the Royal Navy, the scientists requested that Cook command an expedition.

Cook's Voyages

The First Voyage Cook's first major expedition took place from 1768 to 1771. The first objective was astronomical. Scientists on board were to watch the movement of the planet Venus as it passed in front of the sun. They had to make their observations from Tahiti, where the transit could be seen best. The second objective was a secret until Cook was out at sea. He was to sail south to try to find a large continent that many thought was hidden in the South Pacific. It was called Terra Australis Incognita, or "Unknown Southern Land." (This land had nothing to do with Australia, which was already known about though not fully explored.)

The three-year trip failed to find the mythical continent, but Cook achieved some successes.

- He named Tahiti and its neighbors the Society Islands and claimed them for Great Britain.

- He proved that New Zealand was actually two separate islands and explored them in detail.

- He explored and charted 2,000 miles of the eastern coast of Australia and claimed that land for Great Britain.

The Second Voyage Cook's second voyage set out on July 13, 1772, a year and a day after he returned from the first. He sailed his ship, the *Resolution,* south from the Cape of Good Hope, becoming the first to cross the Antarctic Circle. Ice forced him north, but for the next two years he continued exploring. He searched the southern reaches of the Pacific Ocean during the summer and explored in the Polynesian islands during the winter. At each spot, scientists and artists recorded information about the people, plants, and animals they found.

When Cook returned to Great Britain in 1775, he had completed a journey of more than 70,000 miles. His voyage had buried for good the idea of Terra Australis Incognita. Cook had seen only a vast ocean and many islands. He was showered with honors and hailed as a hero.

The Defeat of Scurvy One reason for Cook's fame was his defeat of the dreaded disease scurvy. Caused by a vitamin deficiency, scurvy had killed many hundreds of sailors over the years. By changing his sailors' diet to rely more on fresh food and citrus fruit and less on pickled meats, Cook saved their lives. Not a single sailor died from scurvy in his three-year-long first voyage—a milestone in oceangoing exploration. He met the same success on his second.

The Third Voyage Rather than retire, Cook set out again, in July 1776—this time to locate the Northwest Passage by finding its outlet in the Pacific. On the way, he became the first European to land at the Hawaiian Islands, which he named the Sandwich Islands after the earl of Sandwich (the head of the Royal Navy). From there, Cook explored near Vancouver Island and along the Aleutians. He sailed through the Bering Strait until ice forced him back. He became convinced that the Northwest Passage—a water route north of North America—did not exist.

Cook returned to the Sandwich Islands to winter, hoping to head north once more when warmer weather finally arrived. But tragedy struck. In a dispute with Hawaiians, Cook was killed.

Cook's usual calm and good judgment failed him in his final days. A dispute over alleged thievery by Hawaiians led to a fight that left the great captain dead.

Cook's Legacy

Had he accomplished nothing else, Cook's conquest of scurvy would have earned him a place in history—at least among thankful sailors. But he also achieved much more.

Cook brought science to exploration. First, he buried the myths of the Northwest Passage and Terra Australis Incognita. Second, he and his scientists made careful observations of where they were and what they saw. He was helped in part by the recent development of new aids to navigation. The sextant could track the stars more accurately than ever before; the chronometer measured time accurately on board ship. Both were crucial to Cook's precise location of his ship's position. Equally important, though, were Cook's discipline of mind and steady seamanship. His many months of exploring in the Pacific opened a new world to Europeans.

Alexander Mackenzie

Mackenzie became the first European man to cross the width of North America north of Mexico.

The Fur Trade

In his last voyage, Captain James Cook explored along the North American coast from the Pacific Northwest to Alaska. That journey ended in Cook's death, but it launched a new era. Cook's sailors had purchased some beaver and other skins from Native Americans. When they reached ports in China, they were able to sell those pelts for huge profits. A new fur trade market—between North America and China—had been opened.

This trade was dominated by British fur companies. Canadian fur companies, who wanted the trade for themselves, were locked in their trading posts in the Canadian interior. One post sat at the edge of Lake Athabasca in modern Alberta, Canada. But the vast territory between that point and the western coast of Canada—as well as the area north to the Arctic Ocean—was totally unknown to the traders. Somehow they needed to learn what lay beyond.

Mackenzie's two expeditions both departed from Fort Chipewyan on Lake Athabasca. First he went north, reaching the Beaufort Sea. Four years later, he headed over the Canadian Rockies to the Pacific Ocean.

Mackenzie and the Rivers

The Canadian traders heard two theories about how to get west. An American explorer said that a river that flowed out of the Great Slave Lake (north of Lake Athabasca) led to the Pacific. A Native American suggested another way. The Peace River, which emptied into Lake Athabasca from the west, flowed to the ocean, he said. It took Alexander Mackenzie, a Scot trained as a clerk, to test both theories.

To the Arctic Mackenzie resolved to test the explorer's route first. On June 3, 1789, he and a small party set out in birchbark canoes on a river that connects Lake Athabasca to the Great Slave Lake.

They reached the Great Slave Lake in just a few days, but the lake was frozen—even though it was June. It took two weeks to get through the ice and another week to find the river they sought, at the lake's westernmost point.

At first the river flowed west, as Mackenzie had desired. But eventually it turned north. As the Rocky Mountains rose to the west of the river, it became clear that their route would never bend to the Pacific. Indeed, in mid-July the group reached the river's mouth on the Beaufort Sea, within the Arctic Circle. They met that sea at a small bay now named for Mackenzie. The river, too, bears his name, but that naming came later. He called the river Disappointment.

To the Pacific After returning to the trading post, Mackenzie traveled to England, where he learned how to measure latitude and longitude. With improved skills, he could give more precise locations of what he found. By May 1793, he was back in Canada and ready to test the second route. He and ten others left Lake Athabasca in a single large canoe. It was specially built to hold the explorers and 3,000 pounds of supplies but

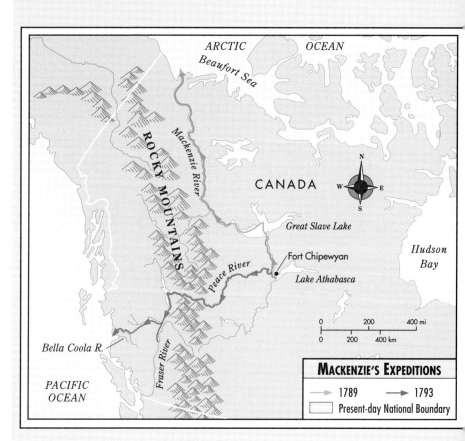

28

still be light enough to carry. They entered the Peace River and headed west.

In less than two weeks, they saw the Rockies, but then strong rapids forced them to leave the river for a while and carry their canoe upstream. At the point where the river forked, Mackenzie took the southerly stream, following it into the mountains.

At the source of that stream, they had to leave the water and carry their canoe 1,000 yards to another river (now called the Fraser). Waterborne again, they headed west. Without realizing it, they had crossed the Continental Divide—the point in the Rockies at which all rivers on the eastern side flow to the east and all rivers on the western side flow to the west. Native Americans had undoubtedly made that crossing before, but Mackenzie and his party were the first white people to do so.

The Fraser proved dangerous. Their canoe wrecked in rapids, they were forced to build a new one. After a few more days of making little progress by water, they decided to travel overland. For 15 days they marched west carrying 90-pound packs. Reaching an Indian village on the Bella Coola River, they were given a feast. From that spot (which Mackenzie called "Friendly Village"), they headed for the coast. Followed by some unfriendly Indians, they marched along the coast for a few days, until Mackenzie decided to leave his mark. He mixed dye with grease and painted a message on a rock overlooking the ocean. It read, "Alexander MacKenzie, from Canada by land, the 22nd of July 1793."

The Mackenzie River, one of the largest in North America, winds its way through the tundra of northern Canada.

Alexander Mackenzie's journal and maps provided information for the explorations of North America that followed.

After Mackenzie

Less well known than Lewis and Clark—who similarly crossed the continent—Mackenzie achieved his feat ten years before them. His drive to succeed can be seen in the decision to improve his skills with knowledge of latitude and longitude and in his careful planning for each trip. For his achievements, he received an English knighthood.

Mackenzie's journal and maps opened large new areas of North America to the knowledge of the white people who were expanding their areas of control. On his heels came more explorers and trappers, as Canadians stretched their country from the Atlantic to the Pacific Coast. Even today much of that land is rough and untraveled. But it is known to us in part because of the great explorations of Alexander Mackenzie.

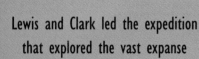

Meriwether Lewis and William Clark

Lewis and Clark led the expedition that explored the vast expanse of land in the Louisiana Purchase.

Meriwether Lewis (left) and William Clark (right), fellow officers and friends, proved to be able leaders for their great journey of exploration.

Three Reasons

U.S. President Thomas Jefferson was both a skilled politician and a lover of knowledge. He was eager to explore the huge landmass to the west of the United States—for more than one reason:

- *Trade.* The British were pushing down from Canada to build their rich fur trade with China. Jefferson wanted some of that profitable trade for the United States. The United States had a trading foothold in Oregon, but it was threatened by British forces in Canada.

- *Security.* With Britain, France, and Spain all having claims to parts of the West, Jefferson wanted to know more about the land and their strength there.

- *Science.* Jefferson simply wanted to know more about the geography, plants, animals, and people in the West.

In a secret message to Congress in 1803, the President proposed an expedition to explore the region. When France agreed to sell the Louisiana Territory to the United States later that year, the idea seemed even better.

The Route West

To carry out these goals, Jefferson chose his friend and personal secretary, a young man named Meriwether Lewis. Lewis chose a co-leader, William Clark, a friend from his army days.

Easy Start Lewis and Clark went to St. Louis, Missouri, where they spent the winter of 1803–1804 preparing for their voyage. They set out from St. Louis on May 14, 1804, with a party of 45.

The first leg of the journey was up the Missouri River to a Mandan Indian village near modern Bismarck, North Dakota. Hindered by the Missouri's strong current, they did not reach the village until November.

The explorers wintered there, forming a friendship with a French

It took two years for Lewis and Clark to cover 8,000 miles. Their work produced the first U.S. map of the route to the Pacific, and their journals informed scientists of hundreds of species unknown before.

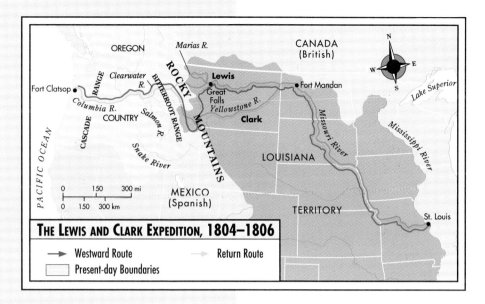

THE LEWIS AND CLARK EXPEDITION, 1804–1806

→ Westward Route   → Return Route
☐ Present-day Boundaries

fur trader named Toussaint Charbonneau and his Indian wife Sacajawea. Lewis invited them along. Sacajawea would be useful as a guide, and her presence would ensure that the party appeared peaceful to other Native Americans they would meet.

Over the Rockies In April 1805, Lewis and Clark headed west with a party of just over 30. (Some of the original group had returned to St. Louis.) The explorers used six new canoes to paddle up the Missouri.

As they neared the Rockies, the going became hard. The river's many rapids forced them to carry their canoes. They found little game, and they began to grow hungry. Soon after reaching the middle of the Rockies, they met a party of Shoshone Indians, whom Sacajawea recognized. They stayed briefly with the tribe—led by Sacajawea's brother—and bought horses to move on.

In September, they were blasted by a mountain snowstorm. Then friendly Nez Percé Indians gave them food. Leaving their horses with the Indians, they returned to newly built canoes to finish their quest.

To the Sea The last run to the Pacific went from the Clearwater River to the Columbia River. They moved

◄ This etching of the Missouri's Great Falls may be based on a sketch Lewis made during the journey.

quickly, sometimes tumbled downstream by rapids. Finally they saw the ocean on November 7. Weakened by hunger and seasick from rough water on the river, they had reached their goal.

Harsh Winter They arrived too late in the year to find any fur-trading ships to transport them back east and too late to return over the mountains. So they had to winter in crude shelters near modern Astoria, Oregon. Constant cold, frequent rain, and little food made it a wretched winter.

Back Home The party left for home in March 1806. At the Nez Percé village, they retrieved their horses. More important, they were given adequate supplies of food. From there, they retraced their steps. Lewis and Clark each led side trips to explore different rivers, but the parties reassembled and finished their journey together.

On September 23, 1806—more than two years after leaving—they returned to St. Louis. Their return amazed everyone, who thought they had all died. In their 8,000-mile trek, though, only one man had died.

After Lewis and Clark

The epic journey of the two explorers changed the face of the United States. Fur trappers began to spread throughout the Rockies. These "mountain men" helped establish a firm American presence in a land that the United States did not yet own. Towns sprang up and eventually became major cities, such as Omaha, Nebraska, and Wichita, Kansas. The British were forced back into Canada, and Oregon and Washington became territories of the United States—as did Montana, Idaho, and the Dakotas.

Lewis and Clark's journals fulfilled Jefferson's desire for more knowledge as well. Their pages told of more than 200 plants and 122 animals previously unknown. They described more than 50 tribes of Native Americans, many of whom had not been met before. Sketches and drawings formed the basis of the first map of the American West. In these journals, Lewis and Clark were also the first to use a now common term for the vast grasslands of the central United States—the Great Plains.

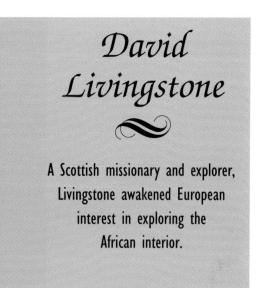

David Livingstone

A Scottish missionary and explorer, Livingstone awakened European interest in exploring the African interior.

A missionary, Livingstone devoted his life to exploring the interior of Africa, in part to help end the slave trade. He was a keen observer and recorded everything he saw. His journals are still being studied by scholars today.

Africa and Livingstone

Europeans and Africa By the middle of the 19th century, Europeans knew a great deal about Africa's coast. It had been explored thoroughly, and trading towns dotted its length. At some of those sites, the trade was in human cargo. The Portuguese and Arabs conducted a lively slave trade on both coasts. But the interior of the continent was largely unknown to Europeans.

Europeans wanted to increase their knowledge of Africa. Many saw economic benefits there. They wanted to seize Africa's rich resources or to promote trade. Others had two goals for the Africans they met. They wanted to teach them the benefits of European civilization and to "save their souls" by converting them to Christianity.

Livingstone the Man Born in Scotland and trained in medicine, David Livingstone shared the desire to convert Africans to Christianity. When he went to Africa for the first time in 1840, at the age of 27, his object was to establish new missions. But he became fascinated by the people, plants, and animals of the continent. He spent most of his next 33 years exploring its interior, with two aims. Not only did he want to expand European knowledge of African geography, he also hoped that, once the African interior was opened to European influence, Europeans could put an end to the slave trade.

To achieve these aims, Livingstone sacrificed his family life. On one trip, he brought along his pregnant wife and three very young children. On a later journey he buried his wife in Africa. Afterward, he returned to England to see a five-year-old daughter for the first time. He suffered illness for years, finally dying at the age of 60—still exploring.

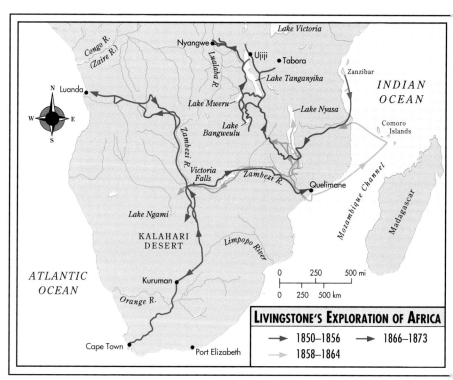

Livingstone's famous meeting with Henry Morton Stanley took place at Ujiji, during his last expedition. He died in a village near Lake Bangweulu.

Livingstone's Explorations

Livingstone began his African career trying to establish new missions to spread the word of Christianity. From 1841 to 1849, he started three new missions. In these early years he became the first European to see Lake Ngami in south central Africa. This discovery, perhaps, awakened the desire to explore farther. From 1850 to his death in 1873, Livingstone undertook three great expeditions.

First Expedition

On his first trip, from 1850 to 1856, he broke new ground:

- He mapped the Zambezi River in its previously uncharted course through the African interior.
- He crossed Africa's interior from Luanda on the Atlantic coast to Quelimane on the Indian Ocean. Although this crossing had been made before, Livingstone's was the first to become widely known in Europe.
- He found the great falls of the Zambezi, which he named Victoria Falls, after Queen Victoria of Britain.

Second Expedition

Already famous from his first journey, Livingstone persuaded the British government to back another expedition. On this trip, which lasted from 1858 to 1864, he tried to explore the Zambezi farther. His main achievement on this voyage was finding Lake Nyasa (also called Lake Malawi).

The Zambezi River drops 343 feet at Victoria Falls, almost twice the height of Niagara Falls in North America.

Third Expedition

David Livingstone's third African trek lasted from 1866 to 1873. Like many who explored in Africa, he was seeking the source of the Nile River. Believing the river began in Lake Tanganyika, he explored around the lake.

This trip is best known not for Livingstone's work, but for another adventurer who found him. After years of hearing nothing from him, all Europe and America assumed that he was dead. A New York newspaper sent a reporter, Henry Morton Stanley, to find Livingstone. After months of travel, Stanley greeted him with the now famous words, "Dr. Livingstone, I presume?" It was the news story of the decade. After they explored together for two months, Stanley asked Livingstone to return with him. The old man refused, wishing to continue his exploring. A little over a year later, he died.

Livingstone's Legacy

Livingstone did more than any other person to lure Europeans to Africa. His detailed notes about land, people, plants, and animals taught Europeans much about what had been a mysterious continent. His writings against the slave trade helped raise opposition to the practice.

But in its place came exploitation of another sort. European powers divided Africa up into colonies that they controlled for decades.

Many Africans understood Livingstone's worth. When he died, his African companions carried his body 900 miles—a journey of nine months—to the coast. There it was transported to England. Before beginning this last journey, they removed Livingstone's heart. It was buried under a tree in an African village, a fitting resting place for the heart of the great explorer.

Richard Francis Burton
and
John Hanning Speke

Two English colleagues turned enemies fought bitterly over the question of the source of the Nile.

Richard Francis Burton (above) is shown dressed as an Arab, a technique he used to travel unharmed in Muslim lands. John Hanning Speke (right), far more conservative in manner, was obsessed with finding the source of the Nile.

The Mystery of the Nile

To 19th-century Europeans, the Nile River of Africa was both familiar and mysterious. The mightiest river of the ancient world, it was well known for centuries. Its waters had nurtured one of the world's earliest and most spectacular civilizations. But the imagination of Europeans was captivated by a great question: Where did the Nile originate? What spot was the source of this famous river?

The Nile is formed by two mighty feeder rivers, the Blue Nile and the White Nile. In 1770, an explorer found the source of the Blue Nile—Lake Tana in present-day Ethiopia. By the 1850s, however, the source of the White Nile was still unknown. Explorers had worked their way upstream as far as Gondokoro, in present-day Sudan. But the way to the source was blocked from that point by difficult country. Another approach was needed.

Ready to step in were two British Army officers. Richard Francis Burton and John Hanning Speke had a novel approach. They planned to find the source by crossing overland, east to west, from the Indian Ocean coast.

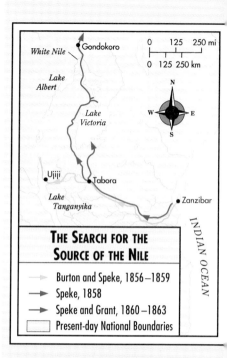

Speke's 1860–1863 expedition led him to the correct conclusion about the Nile's source: It begins at Lake Victoria.

The Journey and the Debate

Burton and Speke were hired by the Royal Geographical Society to undertake the quest. The two had very different personalities. Burton was dashing and impulsive. In his travels, he often dressed like the natives of the region, which was unusual for officers of the British Army. He even disguised himself and traveled to the Muslim holy cities of Mecca and Medina. This trick broke Muslim holy law. Burton was interested in people and languages, of which he spoke many.

Speke was a more traditional British officer. Most important, he was consumed with a passion to find the source of the Nile.

The Journey With Burton in command, the exploring party headed west from Zanzibar (in modern Tanzania). The first leg of the journey took its toll: Burton fell prey to malaria;

Speke suffered another tropical disease that left him temporarily blind.

Still, they were determined to continue. They marched west to the village of Ujiji, on the shore of Lake Tanganyika. This had been their goal, but because of their ill health they could not explore it fully. They trekked back to a village now called Tabora (in Tanzania) to recuperate.

Here the explorers' mutual dislike began. Speke recovered from his illness more quickly and set off to investigate reports of an even larger lake to the north of Tabora. On August 3, 1858, he saw the vast lake. Africans called it Lake Ukerewe. Speke named it Lake Victoria after his queen. Certain that he had found the source of the Nile, he didn't explore any farther.

Excited, Speke told Burton the news—but Burton didn't believe him. He was convinced that Lake Tanganyika was the source.

The Debate The two explorers headed back to England, each angry with the other. When Burton was forced to delay his return due to sickness, Speke reached their home country alone. He announced his belief, which angered Burton further. The head of the Royal Geographical Society agreed with Speke and funded another expedition.

Speke's next trip, with James Augustus Grant (another army officer), explored the lake more fully. They found a large waterfall that poured into a river at the lake's northern end.

Convinced that the waterfall was the source of the Nile, Speke and Grant marched north. Unfortunately, they did not always keep the river in sight on the way to Gondokoro. This failure prevented Speke from proving beyond doubt that he had found the true source.

Meanwhile, Burton maintained that Lake Tanganyika was the source. A great debate was scheduled in September 1864 in England. Burton and Speke were to present their opposing views at a public meeting. The day before the debate, Speke accidentally shot and killed himself in a hunting accident. The official debate was canceled, but the talk didn't stop. Burton's followers proclaimed that Speke's death was the suicide of a man who knew he was in error. Speke's champions called it a tragic accident.

Speke made many sketches during his journeys, depicting the African landscape and wildlife.

After Burton and Speke

The question of the Nile's source remained unsettled. Speke had been correct—Lake Victoria was the source. Unfortunately, he had been so sure of this view that he neglected to find proofs that would convince doubters.

In 1864, explorers Samuel White Baker and his wife Henrietta found that the river issuing from Lake Victoria flowed to another lake. The Bakers called it Lake Albert after Queen Victoria's husband. They then found where the White Nile flowed out of Lake Albert on its route to the Mediterranean Sea.

Even the Bakers' findings did not settle the issue completely. It took two expeditions by Henry Morton Stanley to prove that Lake Victoria was the source of the Nile. Stanley's last journey came in 1890. After that, there was no further doubt that Speke had been right.

John McDouall Stuart

Stuart forged a trail through the center of Australia, a route followed to lay a telegraph line that linked Australia's north and south.

John McDouall Stuart had already explored parts of Australia for almost 15 years when he took up the challenge of crossing the continent from south to north.

Reaching what he called Central Mount Sturt, Stuart planted a flag marking the point as the center of Australia.

The Harsh Australian Interior

In the middle of the 19th century, the Australian interior was largely unknown. Expansion was hampered by the harsh geography of this region. Rugged mountains and hot deserts made natural barriers for travelers. Even the rivers hindered explorers. The rivers of the interior wandered aimlessly, became streams, and then vanished in the desert.

But the government wanted to lay a telegraph line linking Australia from the settled south to the Gulf of Carpentaria in the north. Transoceanic cables could then join the continent by telegraph to India. In 1860, the Parliament of South Australia backed this desire with money. They offered a £2,000 reward to anyone who could cross this harsh land from south to north. A rival provincial government, from Victoria, tried to beat South Australia to the goal.

To achieve these goals, two major expeditions set out in 1860. Both succeeded, but one had a more lasting effect.

Crossing the Continent

Burke and Wills The Victoria expedition was well equipped but poorly led by Robert O'Hara Burke. Leaving the southern port of Melbourne on August 20, 1860, the expedition reached the town of Menindee in October. Opposed by some members of the party, Burke decided to continue with a smaller group. He took with him surveyor William John Wills and three others.

About three and a half weeks later, they reached Cooper Creek, halfway to their goal. Burke left one of the men with supplies and set out again with Wills and two others.

The way was rugged, and it took until mid-February for the three to reach swamps on the shore of the Gulf of Carpentaria. The marsh prevented them from reaching the ocean water, but they had met success.

The return journey was harrowing. Held up by torrential rains and short on supplies, the three travelers trekked home. They had to kill a camel and a horse for food. In mid-April, one man died, leaving Burke, Wills, and John King. A few days later, they reached the storage depot on Cooper Creek to find that the man left there had departed—eight hours before.

Leaving Cooper Creek, the three travelers lost their way. A month after leaving it, they found themselves back at the same spot. By now, they had killed and eaten the remaining camels. After another month of travel, they were pushed beyond endurance. Burke and Wills died sometime in late June of 1861. King was saved by aborigines (native Australians).

Stuart John McDouall Stuart undertook the quest to cross the continent for the South Australia Parliament. Although Burke and Wills were the first to reach the northern coast, Stuart's later success was more lasting. But it took Stuart three attempts to reach his goal.

His first journey, with two companions, began in March 1860. Rapid progress brought them to a mountain about 125 miles north of Alice Springs. The mountain was the geographic

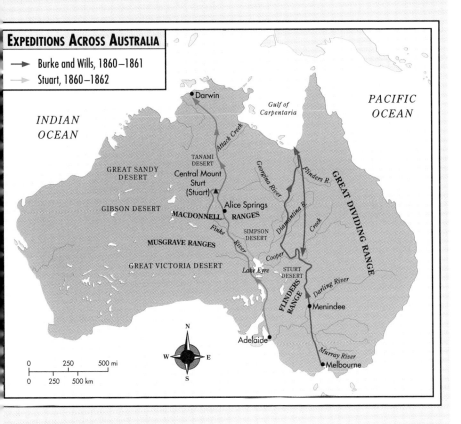

Burke and Wills crossed Australia from south to north toward the east but died on their return. Stuart crossed the continent through its center. He survived the journey, but his health suffered.

Linking Australia

Burke and Wills won first place in the great race to the north. But Stuart's route played a more important role in Australian history. Within nine years of his return, a transcontinental telegraph line was laid. It stretched from Adelaide, his departure point in the south, to Darwin, a northern port near the point where Stuart reached the sea. From there, a cable linked Australia to India, and the rest of the world.

Later, a railroad and a road were also built following Stuart's route. His contribution to knowledge of the Australian interior is now recognized in the name of the mountain he found north of Alice Springs. The name has been changed to Central Mount Stuart.

center of Australia. Stuart named it Central Mount Sturt, after explorer Charles Sturt, with whom he had begun his career.

From there, the trio marched another 175 miles north to a place called Attack Creek. Finally a shortage of supplies, scurvy, and attacks by aborigines drove them back. They reached safety on September 1, 1860.

Stuart's next attempt left from the area around Lake Eyre on January 11, 1861. By April 25, his party had reached Attack Creek again. Another 100 miles of progress were made, but again the party was forced back by lack of food and water.

The third attempt began in October 1861—one month after Stuart's return from his second try. Nine months later, in July of 1862, he reached the Indian Ocean. Wading in, Stuart washed his face and hands in the sea he had endured so much to reach.

Stuart returned a hero, but terribly weakened. Two and a half years of travel had left him stricken by scurvy and night blindness. He was so weak that he had to be carried on a stretcher. He won the prize (plus an additional £1,000) but died within four years. Only 51 at the time, he had never recovered from his epic journey.

The trail that Stuart blazed across the outback—rural Australia—became the route of a railroad that linked the northern and southern coasts.

Sven Hedin

Hedin explored vast regions of central Asia and the Middle East, adding much to geographers' knowledge with his careful records.

Explorer in Training

Sven Hedin, born in Sweden in 1865, was destined to travel to the hottest and coldest regions of the world. A good student, he seems to have been interested in geography and languages early. These two areas of study would serve him well in later years.

At 20, he was hired by a Swedish engineer living in Baku, on the Caspian Sea, to tutor his son. Hedin became exposed to the Middle East and central Asia. Exploring those regions would become his life's work.

In the late 19th century, European maps still left blank vast areas in this part of the world. "Unexplored," they said. Indeed, no more was known of these lands than had been learned from the voyage of Marco Polo. Forty years of travel by Hedin changed that.

The Himalayas—the highest mountains in the world—were the object of Hedin's work in his third expedition.

Hedin's Work

To prepare for his explorations, Hedin learned local languages such as Persian and Tartar. Later, he studied geography at Swedish and German universities. After a stint as an interpreter, he traveled part of the old Silk Road through Tashkent and Samarkand to the Chinese city of Kashi. A few more years of study in Germany, and he was ready to begin his life's work.

From 1894 to 1897 The first expedition was small—just Hedin himself and three Kirghiz companions. (Kirghizia is a region of central Asia.)

First they had to cross the icy Pamir Mountains, east of Tashkent.

One of the great travelers of world history, Sven Hedin journeyed thousands of miles, crossing both burning deserts and frigid mountain passes.

After experiencing extreme cold, they then suffered the scorching heat of the great Takla Makan Desert. One companion was lost in the desert. Hedin and the others barely escaped dying of thirst. They returned to Kashi to recuperate, then set out again in December 1895.

This time skirting the desert to the south, Hedin found a shallow lake called Lop Nur. He determined that this was a famous lake that ancient Chinese records called the "Wandering Lake," because the shifting desert changed its shape.

After a brief rest in April 1896, Hedin set out again. This time he marched all the way across Asia to Beijing. To get there, he had to cross the great Gobi Desert, much of which he mapped for the first time.

From 1899 to 1902 Awarded a gold medal by the Swedish king for

The palace of the Dalai Lama sits high in the Tibetan mountains in the sacred city of Lhasa, which Hedin tried to enter.

his triumph, Hedin simply prepared to set out again. His next expedition explored one of the rivers that girded the Takla Makan Desert. In his travels, he found the remains of an ancient city named Lou-lan. The city was 1,800 years old.

This journey was cut short when Hedin was caught trying to enter the sacred city of Lhasa in Tibet. The ruler of Tibet, the Dalai Lama, had forbidden westerners from seeing Lhasa. Hedin was forced to return home.

From 1906 to 1908 He didn't remain home for long. His next journey took him to the great Himalaya Mountains. Hedin mapped mountains and valleys and passes that had never been charted before. In honor of his achievement, this spiny region now bears his name—the Hedin Transhimalayas.

In the course of this work, Hedin also followed two of India's great rivers to their sources. He carefully traced the beginnings of both the Indus and the Brahmaputra, again providing accurate details about areas that had been called unknown.

Later Travels For almost 20 years, Hedin remained in Europe writing up the results of his explorations. From 1926 through 1935 (when he was in his 60s), he journeyed through central Asia again.

In the first years of this period, he led a large group of scientists who made detailed studies of the land, water, plants, and animals of the northwestern provinces of China. The results of this research were published in more than 50 volumes. In the last years of this span, Hedin mapped the old Silk Road for the Chinese government.

Hedin's Contribution

Hedin's achicvements were remarkable. He traveled thousands of miles creating accurate maps of previously unexplored regions. These areas had been considered for centuries as part of the "known world." Yet numerous question marks about them remained until Hedin's labors solved many of the mysteries.

Hedin achieved these feats in spite of facing the harshest of geographic obstacles. He climbed the cold Pamirs and the frigid Himalayas with their thin air. He crossed the huge arid expanses of the Takla Makan and Gobi deserts. His first accounts of these travels were aimed at a popular audience and triggered great European interest in the regions. Later, Hedin turned to detailed scientific studies, which have helped scientists and historians learn about the geography, natural science, and past of the areas.

Robert Peary

Peary endured bitter cold and endless ice to become the first explorer to reach the North Pole.

Call to Adventure

Some explorers have been moved by the desire for riches, others by science, and still others by an urge to fill in blank areas on the map. Robert Peary simply wanted the glory of being the first person to reach the North Pole. Obsessed by what he called "Arctic fever," he was determined to win that race.

Peary was not the first explorer to be obsessed by the same idea. A Swede named Salomon Andrée tried to reach the pole in a balloon. George Washington De Long, an American, and Fridtjof Nansen, a Norwegian, both tried using ships.

These attempts failed. Andrée's balloon lost its steering gear and went down; he and his three companions died. De Long's ship was trapped in the ice and crushed. Nansen's ship survived the ice, but the explorer never reached the pole. It became clear that ships could not be used because the ice around the pole was permanent. The only way to reach the pole was over that ice.

Peary's Success

Peary's Advantages To reach his goal, Peary wisely adopted the ways of the Inuit (often called Eskimos). He traveled with sleds pulled by dog teams. His rations consisted of pemmican (dried meat), condensed milk, tea, and hardtack (flour-and-water biscuits). He used igloos as shelters along the way.

Peary was able to succeed by using a strategy of support teams that prepared the way for the final approach. He would send groups of men and dogs ahead to make camps. They would leave supplies and return; then another group would go farther and deposit another cache of supplies. This way the final team, aiming to reach the pole, could travel fairly light and make good speed along the ice.

Peary was also a skillful promoter—of himself and of his quest. He generated public interest in his plan and was able to secure the support of a number of wealthy people. Forming the Peary Arctic Club in 1897, they financed his expeditions and used their influence to get the U.S. Navy, Peary's employer, to grant him leave to go on these expeditions. The Arctic Club even built Peary a specially designed ship, the *Roosevelt*.

Perhaps one of Peary's greatest assets was Matthew Henson, originally his servant but in the end a fellow adventurer. Henson, an African American, accompanied Peary on most of his expeditions. He became a skilled sled driver and a reliable companion. Henson was the only non-Inuit to accompany Peary on his final dash to the pole.

Despite good planning and reliable help, Peary's expeditions were not without difficulties. The Arctic is a dangerous region, where temperatures can reach –60° F. On one trip Peary lost some toes on one foot—frozen, they had broken off when his boot was removed. Leads, or breaks in the ice, presented danger and delayed progress by forcing the explorers to go around them or wait for them to freeze.

Peary, in a photo taken aboard his ship, is well prepared for the bitter cold of the Arctic.

Once Peary's party reached the pole, the paused for a celebratory photograph.

Final Victory In the 1880s and 1890s, Peary learned his skills in Arctic travel by sledding across Greenland. (His travels here helped prove that Greenland is an island.) An expedition in 1905–1906 moved him within 186 miles of the pole, but he was forced to turn back. (It was during this journey that Peary lost his toes.) In July 1908 he sailed in the *Roosevelt* for his final assault. Now 52, Peary believed that this was his last chance.

The expedition went smoothly. The ship took on many Inuit and over 200 dogs and then proceeded north. The *Roosevelt*'s captain pushed it to Cape Columbia, at the northern shore of Ellesmere Island, northwest of Greenland, 420 miles from the pole.

Starting on March 1, 1909, Peary began to send the supply parties ahead. Shortly afterward, Peary and Henson set out with their four Inuit sledders. Peary's party was stopped by a wide lead that opened in the ice; it took six days to freeze over and permit passage. On March 19, one group was sent back.

By April 1, the party was only 133 miles from the pole. Peary sent back the remaining teams, leaving only himself, Henson, four Inuit, and 40 dogs. On April 4, they reached 89°, 57′ North—3 minutes in latitude from the pole. After a rest, Peary and two Inuit pushed over the pole and reached 89°, 55′ North. Peary had crossed the top of the world.

Rival Claims

The *Roosevelt* returned to New York with Peary expecting a hero's welcome. Imagine his surprise when he learned that another explorer, Dr. Frederick A. Cook, claimed to have reached the pole the year before! Cook, however, offered no proof and his claim was widely discredited, whereas Peary did become the popularly accepted conqueror of the pole.

Even Peary has his doubters, though. Some scholars say that his writings provide insufficient proof that he did indeed reach the pole. Others back his claim. Still he is widely accepted as having been the first.

In the end, Peary enjoyed the fame that he had sought. A number of his books sold well. He was widely acclaimed by the public. The U.S. Congress voted him the pension of a rear admiral—although he never held such a high rank.

Peary used dog sleds like this one to travel over the frozen wastes of the North. His companion and friend Matthew Henson became a skilled sledder.

Roald Amundsen

Amundsen was the first explorer to reach the South Pole and the first to travel to both the North and South poles.

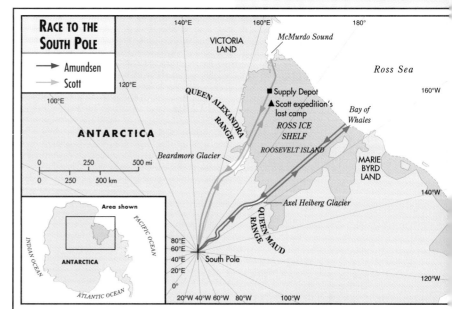

Roald Amundsen was a skilled polar explorer and brilliant organizer.

The Lure of the Arctic

As a boy in Norway, Roald Amundsen had read of the failed expedition of Sir John Franklin. In the 1840s, Franklin had tried to navigate through the icy waters of the Arctic Ocean to find the Northwest Passage from the Atlantic to the Pacific. Franklin's ship was trapped in ice, and he and 129 crew members died. The story captivated Amundsen's imagination and led him to become an Arctic explorer.

The Northwest Passage, which was Amundsen's first goal, had long been sought as a commercial route. By the middle of the 19th century, people realized that the route was too icy and dangerous to have any real commercial value. But Amundsen still wanted to conquer the frigid waters—simply to say that it had been done. His desire to be first in achieving difficult goals would lead him to undertake four great expeditions during his life. These expeditions took him to both ends of the earth. One cost him his life.

Amundsen's base at the Bay of Whales put him closer to the South Pole than Scott, helping him reach that goal first.

Amundsen's Expeditions

Sailing the Northwest Passage In June 1903, Amundsen set out to attempt the Northwest Passage. His departure from Oslo was not promising; he slipped out at midnight to escape from creditors to the expedition, who wanted repayment of their loans.

Because ice on the Arctic Ocean was less of a problem than in most years, the ship proceeded easily at first. Briefly halted when the ship grounded, the crew got it afloat again and reached a harbor on King William Island. After two years there, they departed in August 1905. Sighting a ship that had come from the Bering Strait, they knew that they had found a route to the Pacific.

But ice forced them to spend another winter in the Arctic. Not until 1906 could they pass through the Bering Strait and into the Pacific Ocean. The ship reached San Francisco in October 1906. Having sent advance word of his success, Amundsen was received as a hero.

> ## "We shall stick it out to the end, but we are getting weaker, of course, and the end cannot be far. It seems a pity, but I do not think I can write more."

In these moving words, Scott penned his last thoughts before dying. His journal was found when his body was discovered.

The Race to the South Pole Back in Norway, Amundsen planned an attempt to reach the North Pole by sea. As preparations were underway, Robert Peary announced that he had reached the pole.

Though disappointed, Amundsen set a new goal—to be the first to reach the South Pole. He knew that the English explorer Robert Falcon Scott was planning such a journey. Amundsen feared that if he revealed his plans, Scott would speed up his own preparations. Therefore, Amundsen kept his new destination secret.

Stopping at the Madeira Islands off Spain, Amundsen finally announced his plan. Scott, angered at the competition, did speed his preparations while Amundsen continued to Antarctica. The race was on.

Amundsen landed at the Bay of Whales off the Ross Sea. That put him about 70 miles closer to the pole than would Scott's base in McMurdo Sound.

Amundsen spent the winter of 1911 advancing partway to leave caches of supplies. On October 19, 1911 (which is spring in the Southern Hemisphere), he set out with four fellow explorers and four sledges with 13 dogs each.

As they traveled, Amundsen took a controversial step. As the party advanced and food was consumed, fewer dogs were needed. Amundsen had the extra dogs killed; then he and the others in his party (as well as the remaining dogs) ate them.

With his head start, shorter route, and some good luck, Amundsen reached the pole first, arriving on December 14, 1911. He left a letter to the king of Norway, asking Scott to carry it back, in case he died on the return trip.

But Amundsen survived; it was Scott who died. He and four companions reached the pole a month after Amundsen. They died in March 1912, after a grueling return trip. Their frozen bodies were not discovered until November 1912. They were within 11 miles of a supply depot. Scott still had Amundsen's letter to the king.

Flying North Amundsen's next adventure was in the 1920s. Convinced that air travel provided a key to conquering the North Pole, he planned to fly a dirigible over it. Another race developed, this time with the American Richard Byrd. Amundsen lost this race. Byrd, using a plane, reached the pole on May 9, 1926. Amundsen's airship passed over it three days later. Still, the trip gave Amundsen the distinction of being the first explorer to reach both poles.

The Aftermath

Bitter public disagreements followed the voyage of the airship. Amundsen attacked its designer and pilot, the Italian Umberto Nobile. When Nobile attempted another polar flyover in 1928, his new airship crashed. Amundsen buried the ill feelings to join in rescue efforts. Nobile was found by another party, but Amundsen died when his plane went down in the Arctic Ocean.

Amundsen's rescue attempt restored his reputation, which had suffered from the quarrel with Nobile. In truth, he had achieved much:

- He was the first to navigate the long-sought Northwest Passage.
- Measurements he took on that voyage helped fix the true location of the north magnetic pole.
- He was the first to reach the South Pole.

Exploration of this planet continued. But within 40 years of Amundsen's death, exploration of new uncharted regions—the solar system—had begun.

Freezing waters, jagged rocks, icy land, and frigid temperatures all present harsh challenges to Antarctic travelers.

43

Glossary

aborigines: The native peoples of any area.

airship: An aircraft with a large bladder filled with gas that is lighter than air, a motor, and a steering mechanism; also called a dirigible, zeppelin, or blimp.

cache: A deposit of supplies or weapons left in a safe and hidden place.

calumet: The Native American ceremonial tobacco pipe, which was shared at meetings by leaders of different groups to signal their peaceful intentions toward one another.

caravan: A group of people traveling together; used to refer to groups of merchants crossing deserts.

Cathay: The name used by Europeans of the Middle Ages to refer to China.

circumnavigation: A trip around the world by water.

colonialism: A nation's policy of extending control over the people of foreign lands.

epidemic: The outbreak and rapid spread of an infectious disease.

estuary: The wide lower area of a river where the river water meets the ocean's tides.

expedition: A journey undertaken to achieve a specific goal.

hardtack: A hard biscuit made only with flour and water.

igloo: A structure made of tightly fitted blocks of snow or ice; developed by the Inuit people of Arctic North America.

Indies: The name given by Europeans to groups of islands in the southern Pacific (the East Indies) and the Caribbean Sea (the West Indies), which were both the objects of many voyages of exploration.

Inuit: A Native American people of the Arctic.

Jesuits: Catholic priests belonging to a particular religious order, renowned for their learning and their missionary zeal.

latitude and longitude: The two imaginary sets of lines (latitude running east and west and longitude north and south) used to create a grid system on the earth for geographers and others to accurately plot locations; measured in degrees, minutes, and seconds; the North and South poles are at latitude 90° north and 90° south and the Equator is at latitude 0°.

malaria: An infectious disease common in tropical lands resulting in chills and fever and transmitted by the bite of a mosquito.

missionary: A person who teaches about his or her religion, frequently traveling to a foreign land to do so.

Mongol: A member of a nomadic people of the Gobi Desert who, in the 13th century, conquered China and much of Asia.

Muslim: A believer in the religion of Islam.

mutiny: A rebellion by soldiers or sailors against their commander.

navigation: The art of planning a course on the seas and of making adjustments—to account for the effects of current or wind—to maintain that course.

New France: The area of North America claimed and settled by France, comprising eastern Canada along the St. Lawrence River to the Great Lakes and down the Mississippi River to present-day Louisiana; the northern portion was surrendered to the English after the French and Indian War of the 1750s.

Northeast Passage: The sea route from Europe to Asia to be achieved by sailing east (north of Russia).

Northwest Passage: An open-sea lane from the Atlantic to the Pacific that, for centuries, Europeans believed must exist and tried to find; the true passage was not discovered until the early 20th century; because it is in Arctic waters, often plugged with ice, it is not commercially useful.

peninsula: A long body of land extending into a water area and touched by water on three sides.

portage: To carry boats or goods overland from one waterway to another.

pueblos: Communal dwellings of sunbaked mud constructed by Native Americans in the American Southwest.

rapids: A fast-moving, often rocky stretch of river.

scurvy: A disease caused by a lack of vitamin C in the diet, which produces swollen and bleeding gums, internal bleeding, and weakness; scurvy killed many hundreds of sailors over the centuries until Captain Cook proved that a diet with more fresh food and citrus fruit could prevent the disease.

Siberia: The region in eastern Russia stretching (west to east) from the Ural Mountains to the Pacific Ocean and (north to south) from the Arctic Ocean to the Gobi Desert.

Silk Road: An ancient trade route from China through central Asia to the Black Sea on which Muslim merchants would bring silk, jewels, and spices from Asia for trading in the Mediterranean.

smallpox: A highly infectious disease that causes chills and fever and can cause death; it was known in Europe for centuries before European contact with Native Americans, but because it had not developed in America, Native Americans had no natural immunity to it; thus millions of Native Americans died from it.

spices: Food flavorings such as cinnamon, nutmeg, and peppercorn much prized by Europeans in the Middle Ages and later, which were the object of a rich trade.

strait: A narrow waterway connecting two large bodies of water.

Terra Australis Incognita: Literally, the "Unknown Southern Land," a large continent thought to exist in the southern Pacific but which does not, in fact, exist.

tundra: A treeless region just below the Arctic Circle in which the earth just below the surface is permanently frozen.

voyageurs: The French name for the early French fur traders of North America who also explored along rivers and in forests.

wampum: Small beads made from shells, used by Native Americans for jewelry and money.

Suggested Readings

Note: An asterisk (*) denotes a Young Adult title.

*Anderson, Madelyn K. *Robert E. Peary and the Fight for the North Pole.* Franklin Watts, 1992.

*Brownlee, Walter. *The First Ships Round the World.* Cambridge University Press, 1974.

Coulter, Tony. *Jacques Cartier, Samuel de Champlain, and the Explorers of Canada.* Chelsea House, 1993.

Cox, Isaac J., editor. *The Journeys of René Robert Cavalier.* AMS Press, reprint of 1922 edition.

Day, Arthur G. *Coronado's Quest: The Discovery of the Southwestern States.* Greenwood, 1982.

*Flaherty, Leo, and Goetzmann, William H. *Roald Amundsen and the Quest for the South Pole.* Chelsea House, 1993.

Hing, Robert J. *Tracking Mackenzie to the Sea: Coast to Coast in Eighteen Splashdowns.* Anchor Watch, 1992.

*Hoobler, Dorothy, and Hoobler, Thomas. *The Voyages of Captain Cook.* Putnam, 1983.

Into the Unknown: The Story of Exploration. National Geographic Society, 1987.

Johnson, Donald S. *Charting the Sea of Darkness: The Four Voyages of Henry Hudson.* McGraw-Hill, 1992.

Journals of the Lewis and Clark Expedition. University of Nebraska Press, 1990.

Kish, George. *To the Heart of Asia.* University of Michigan Press, 1984.

Lauridsen, Peter. *Vitus Bering.* Select Bibliographies Reprint Series. Ayer Company Publishers, 1889.

Lavender, David S. *The Way to the Western Sea.* Anchor Books, 1990.

Marrin, Albert. *Aztecs and Spaniards.* Atheneum, 1986.

*Meltzer, Milton. *Columbus and the World Around Him.* Franklin Watts, 1990.

Mirsky, Jeannette. *Westward Crossings: Balboa, Mackenzie, Lewis and Clark.* University of Chicago Press, 1970.

Morison, Samuel Eliot. *The European Discovery of America: The Northern Voyages.* Oxford University Press, 1971.

———. *The European Discovery of America: The Southern Voyages.* Oxford University Press, 1974.

Rice, Edward. *Captain Sir Richard Francis Burton.* Macmillan, 1990.

*Stefoff, Rebecca. *Ferdinand Magellan and the Discovery of the World Ocean.* Chelsea House, 1990.

*———. *Marco Polo and the Medieval Explorers.* Chelsea House, 1992.

*———. *Vasco da Gama and the Portuguese Explorers.* Chelsea House, 1993.

*———. *Women of the World.* Oxford University Press, 1992.

Sugden, John. *Sir Francis Drake.* Touchstone Books, 1990.

Tinling, Marion. *Women into the Unknown: A Sourcebook on Women Explorers and Travelers.* Greenwood Press, 1989.

Wilson, Derek. *The Circumnavigators.* M. Evans and Company, 1989.

Index